A New Zealand
Response to Challenge
The War At Home
RUTH NAUMANN

Contents

1939 – Major crisis

If you were 13 or 14 in 1939 ...

you might be going to work
ery day instead of coming to
hool.

... you would probably have a lot of brothers and sisters.

... you would never have heard of television but your family might be lucky enough to own a radio.

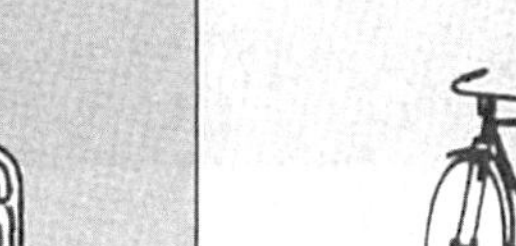

.... you might be very lucky and have your own bike.

your family, especially if you
ed in town, would probably not
n a car.

... you might have been sick some time during your 4th and 10th birthdays when New Zealand had a bad depression and many children did not have enough to eat.

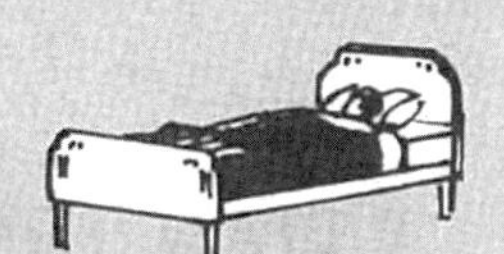

... you and your family would all be looking forward to better times now.

... your mother would probably be a full-time housewife.

your elder unmarried sister
uld probably have a job in a
op or factory or be in domestic
rvice as a servant or waitress.

... your home would probably not have a bathroom or inside toilet. If you lived in town, a night cartman would come into your backyard to empty the bucket from your outside toilet.

... you might have an unmarried relation who has been sent to live in another town because she is having a baby and brought shame to the family.

... you might be living in an area where there is no electricity or gas so your mother does the cooking on a coal range.

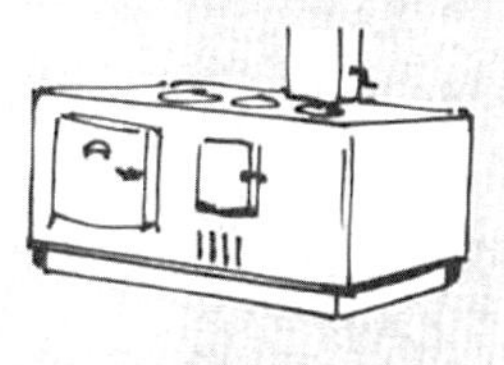

you probably would not have a
ephone in your house.

... you would be living in a country with a population of only 1.5 million.

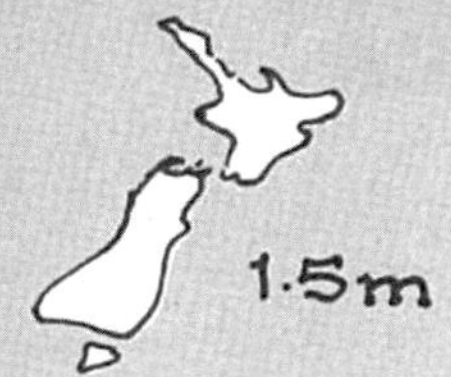

... your home probably would not have a fridge or washing machine.

... you would be judged largely on what your father does and whether you are rich or poor, Maori or European.

you would have been taught
at New Zealand is called a
minion and is part
the British Empire.

... you would have been taught to feel loyal to Britain and to stand up when 'God Save the King' was played at an event like a concert or movie.

... on Father's Day, 3rd September 1939, you may have heard Prime Minister Michael Savage announce...

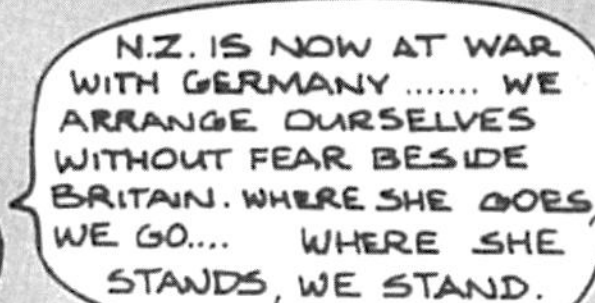

... you would be excited and perhaps run out to your back lawn to watch for Hitler's planes.

WAR **would change New Zealand and it would change your life. Nothing would ever be quite the same again. This war would be one of the greatest challenges that you and your country would have to face.**

How it was a world war

The war of 1939 to 1945 was called the Second World War because so many countries were involved.

This is how the two sides and their main allies (friends) lined up:

	GERMANY	ITALY	JAPAN		BRITAIN	FRANCE	RUSSIA	UNITED STATES
ENTRY	END 1939	MID 1940	END 1941	VERSUS	END 1939 including Dominions like New Zealand	END 1939	MID 1941	END 1941
EXIT	MID 1945	END 1943	END 1945		END 1945	MID 1940	END 1945	END 1945

Years shown on the chart: 1939, 1940, 1941, 1942, 1943, 1944, 1945

Some places New Zealand soldiers went to (standing by, resting, fighting) –

- Egypt
- Greece
- Libya
- Italy
- New Caledonia
- Britain
- Crete
- Syria
- Solomon Islands

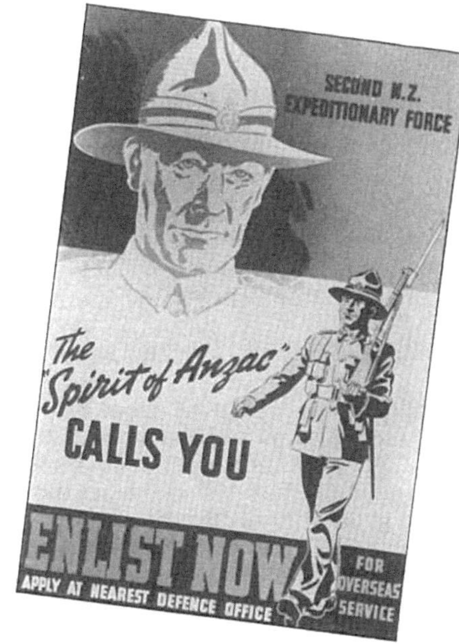

SECOND N.Z. EXPEDITIONARY FORCE
The "Spirit of Anzac" CALLS YOU
ENLIST NOW
FOR OVERSEAS SERVICE
APPLY AT NEAREST DEFENCE OFFICE

Some places New Zealand pilots went to (bomber raids, convoy and escort duties, training) –

- Canada
- New Hebrides
- Bismarck Archipelago
- Germany
- Solomon Islands
- Battle of Britain

Some places New Zealand sailors went to –

- Pacific Ocean
- Atlantic Ocean

Some important ships were –
Achilles, a cruiser in the Battle of River Plate.
Monowai, armed merchant cruiser in escort and patrol duties in Pacific.
Kiwi, *Moa*, *Tui*, minesweepers against enemy submarines in Pacific.
Neptune, sunk in 1941, 150 New Zealanders lost their lives.

The map shows how close the war actually came to New Zealand and why people worried about 'The Yellow Peril'.

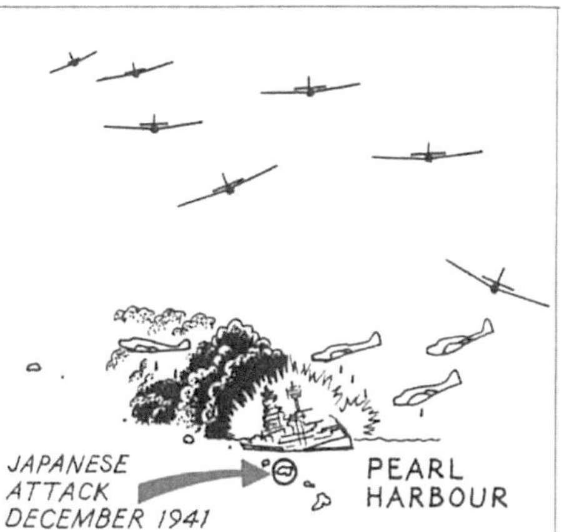

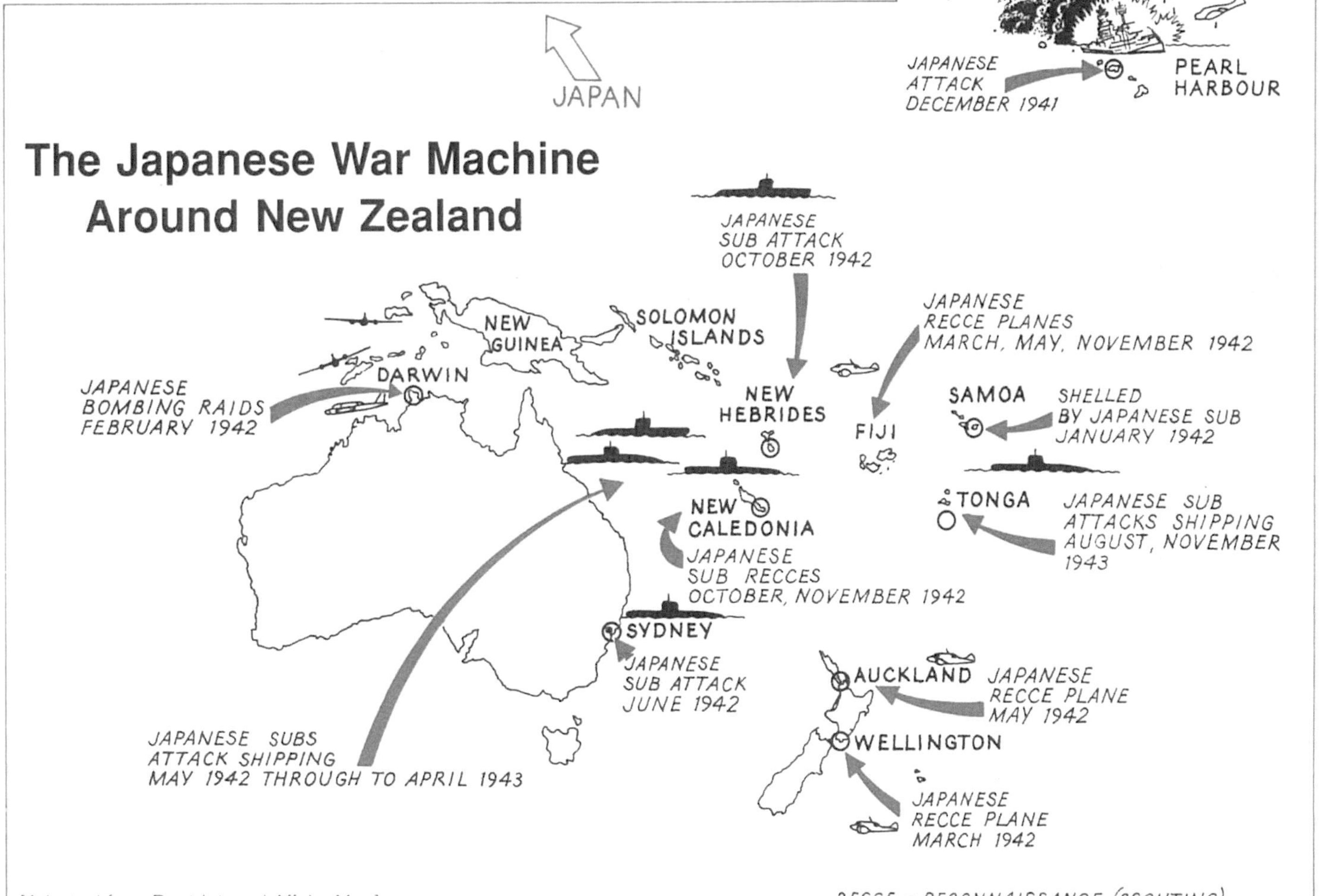
JAPANESE ATTACK DECEMBER 1941
PEARL HARBOUR
JAPAN
The Japanese War Machine Around New Zealand
JAPANESE SUB ATTACK OCTOBER 1942
JAPANESE RECCE PLANES MARCH, MAY, NOVEMBER 1942
NEW GUINEA
SOLOMON ISLANDS
DARWIN
JAPANESE BOMBING RAIDS FEBRUARY 1942
NEW HEBRIDES
FIJI
SAMOA
SHELLED BY JAPANESE SUB JANUARY 1942
TONGA
JAPANESE SUB ATTACKS SHIPPING AUGUST, NOVEMBER 1943
NEW CALEDONIA
JAPANESE SUB RECCES OCTOBER, NOVEMBER 1942
SYDNEY
JAPANESE SUB ATTACK JUNE 1942
AUCKLAND
JAPANESE RECCE PLANE MAY 1942
WELLINGTON
JAPANESE RECCE PLANE MARCH 1942
JAPANESE SUBS ATTACK SHIPPING MAY 1942 THROUGH TO APRIL 1943
RECCE = RECONNAISSANCE (SCOUTING)

[Adapted from Dept Internal Affairs Map]

Hunting a German Raider – An Example of New Zealanders in Action

Name of battle – Battle of the River Plate (Rio de la Plata).

Place – Atlantic Ocean. *See map.*

Prelude – British navy cruisers have been hunting for the German *Admiral Graf Spee* which has just sunk three British ships.

Time – 6.15 a.m. 13th December 1939.

Situation – Smoke is sighted on the horizon; ship is identified as the German pocket battleship *Admiral Graf Spee.* She is a fast and cunning raider with six 11-inch guns and deck armour, far superior to all other cruisers.

The British naval force consists of three cruisers, *Exeter, Ajax* and *Achilles. Achilles* is manned by New Zealanders. *Exeter* has 8-inch guns, *Ajax* and *Achilles* have 6-inch guns.

The Battle – Most of *Graf Spee's* salvos hit *Exeter* which gets severe damage and 61 crew are killed; *Ajax* and *Achilles* pound *Graf Spee's* superstructure, four New Zealand naval ratings are killed and three seriously injured.

Very worried, *Graf Spee* flees for safety to Montevideo which is neutral. *Ajax* and *Achilles* chase. *Graf Spee* enters port to repair damage and report to Hitler. *Ajax* and *Achilles* lie in wait outside the port. British reinforcements go full speed towards them.

Hitler has several choices now to give the captain of the *Admiral Graf Spee*.

Activities

1 See if you can find either a picture, or a model, or the article itself of something from this war-time (1939–1945) list –

- telephone
- bike
- radio
- badge
- flag
- car
- motor cycle
- uniform
- military camp
- military tank

2 Make your own copy of the **Entry/Exit** chart (page 4). Make it 14 cm high. Under the name of each country, put a drawing of their flag or symbol used in the war.

3 Use a full page to copy a map of the world. Use the key to show –

 New Zealand's allies

 New Zealand's enemies

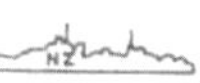 Places New Zealand sailors went to

 Places New Zealand soldiers went to

 Places New Zealand airmen went to

 Japanese planes

 Japanese submarines

Give your map a title and a frame.

4 Choose one place that New Zealanders went to during the war and find out as much as you can about what they did there.

5 Make your own copy or model of the Rio de la Plata. Then make up a list of all the options Hitler had. Decide which one you would have given as an order to the captain of the *Admiral Graf Spee*. Find out who in the class was the closest to what actually happened.

Slit trenches and evacuation drills

As soon as New Zealand was at war, plans had to be made to cope with the challenge.

Soldiers, sailors, airmen had to be organised. New Zealand's army was the Voluntary Territorial Army. The Prime Minister had been pleased with the type of men it had. He said they were getting footballers and young farmers, the pick of New Zealand. These men were immediately mobilised (prepared for fighting) when war broke out. Many others volunteered.

Posters, speeches, bands, parades of weapons and special recruitment drives encouraged other men to enlist in the army. During a football match, for example, a troop of men might march with gaps in their ranks so that men from the crowd could join in.

It was a big decision to make. If a farmer, for example, was killed overseas, the wife would have to think about selling the farm. With some jobs, the home went with the job and if the man was killed, the family would have no home.

Some men lied about their age and the number of children they had so the army would take them. They spoke of 'going to lick the enemy for God, King and country'. Failing the medical test was a big disappointment to many.

Sometimes, the eldest son might get white feathers sent to him. This was a sign of cowardice and he might feel so guilty, he would volunteer, leaving behind a mother, sick father and young brothers and sisters to run a farm. If the 9 or 10 year old brother was caught driving the lorry to the factory, the mother would be taken to court.

Camps had to be built for the soldiers. The largest army camps were at Waiouru and Papakura. It took only two months to build the one at Papakura. More than a thousand men worked 12 hours a day to build 25 acres of dormitories, mess rooms, cook houses, offices, recreation rooms. With its electric light and hot and cold showers, it was real luxury for a lot of men.

New Zealand was not very well equipped to fight off a possible invasion at the beginning of the war. The army advertised for weapons – it wanted .303 and .22 rifles, shotguns, revolvers and ammunition. Women were taught to shoot revolvers. Booby traps were invented. Many camouflage suits and nets were made by the Maori from flax.

A big risk was diseases such as T.B., smallpox and malaria being brought into New Zealand by soldiers coming home. Another big danger was the arrival of malaria-causing mosquitoes. Two men were given the special job of collecting mosquitoes to identify them and carrying out surveys of mosquito breeding places in Wellington and Auckland and around places like aerodromes and ports.

Coastal defences had to be set up in case the enemy sent submarines or planes.

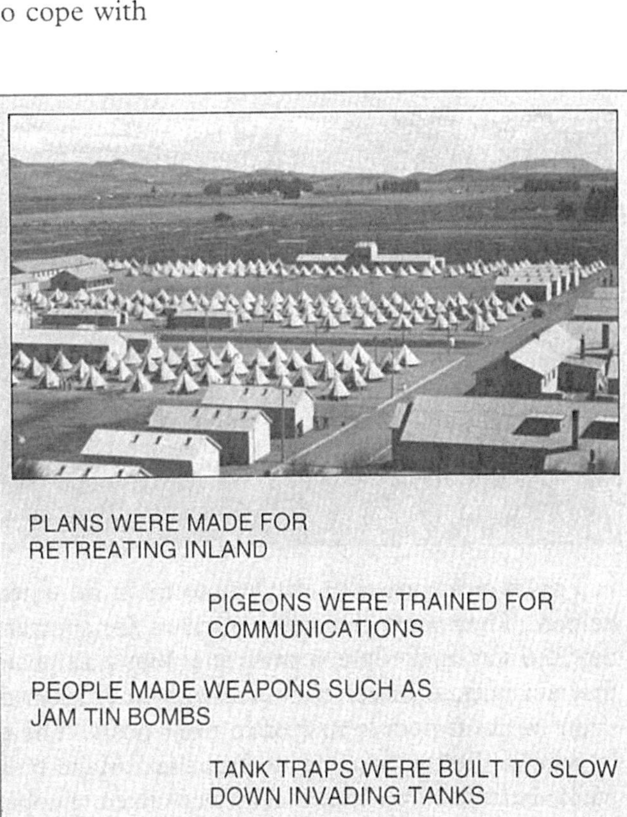

PLANS WERE MADE FOR RETREATING INLAND

PIGEONS WERE TRAINED FOR COMMUNICATIONS

PEOPLE MADE WEAPONS SUCH AS JAM TIN BOMBS

TANK TRAPS WERE BUILT TO SLOW DOWN INVADING TANKS

LIBRARIES AND MUSEUMS HID THEIR TREASURES

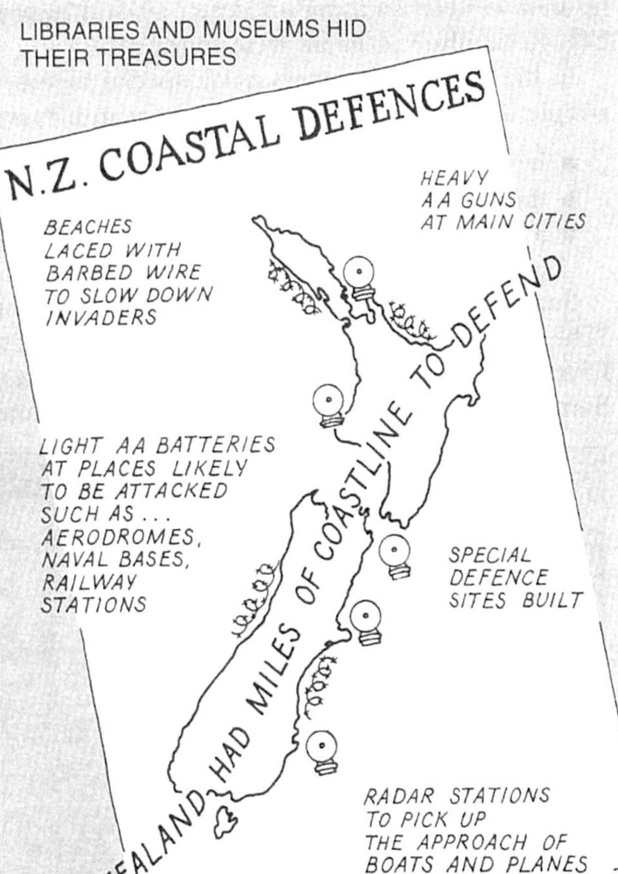

Home-made shelters varied from very simp
to very elaborate.

Towns held practices of what to do in an emergency. School children helped. They were given jobs such as fire spotters or being patients for the Red Cross. People with special jobs had posts to go to, such as a first aid post. All over New Zealand, in cities and tiny towns, when a siren went off people rushed to their posts. The general public was sent to special shelter areas or slit trenches. Make-believe fires were put out. Make-believe water main leaks were fixed. People pretending to be injured were taken away on stretchers and bandaged. Areas where make-believe bombs had fallen were roped off.

In the practices, runners made special reports of damages for the people in charge to deal with. Some examples were:

- a bomb has hit the reservoir and caused a massive flood
- the railway station has been hit and people trapped
- a plane has crashed into a petrol station and a fire is raging.

Some people said the practices were silly and refused to take part. When the siren went off, they kept going about their business while their friends were busy being wounded or dodging machine gun fire. Sometimes, such people were taken to Court and fined.

Activity

This is a list of recommended emergency rations. Sometimes, after spending days deciding what to pack, people found it was too heavy to carry or lift on to the pack-horse.

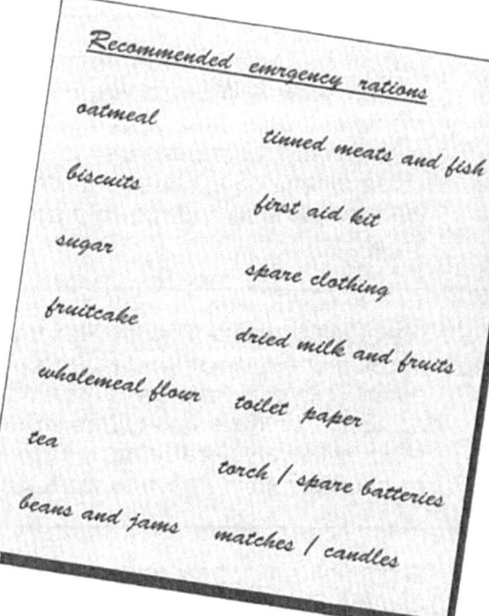

Recommended emergency rations

oatmeal
tinned meats and fish
biscuits
first aid kit
sugar
spare clothing
fruitcake
dried milk and fruits
wholemeal flour
toilet paper
tea
torch / spare batteries
beans and jams
matches / candles

Everyone in your group should bring one item for an emergency war-time rations box, including a box to pack it in. Then pack it, discussing what can be left out if necessary. It has to be light enough for a person to lift.

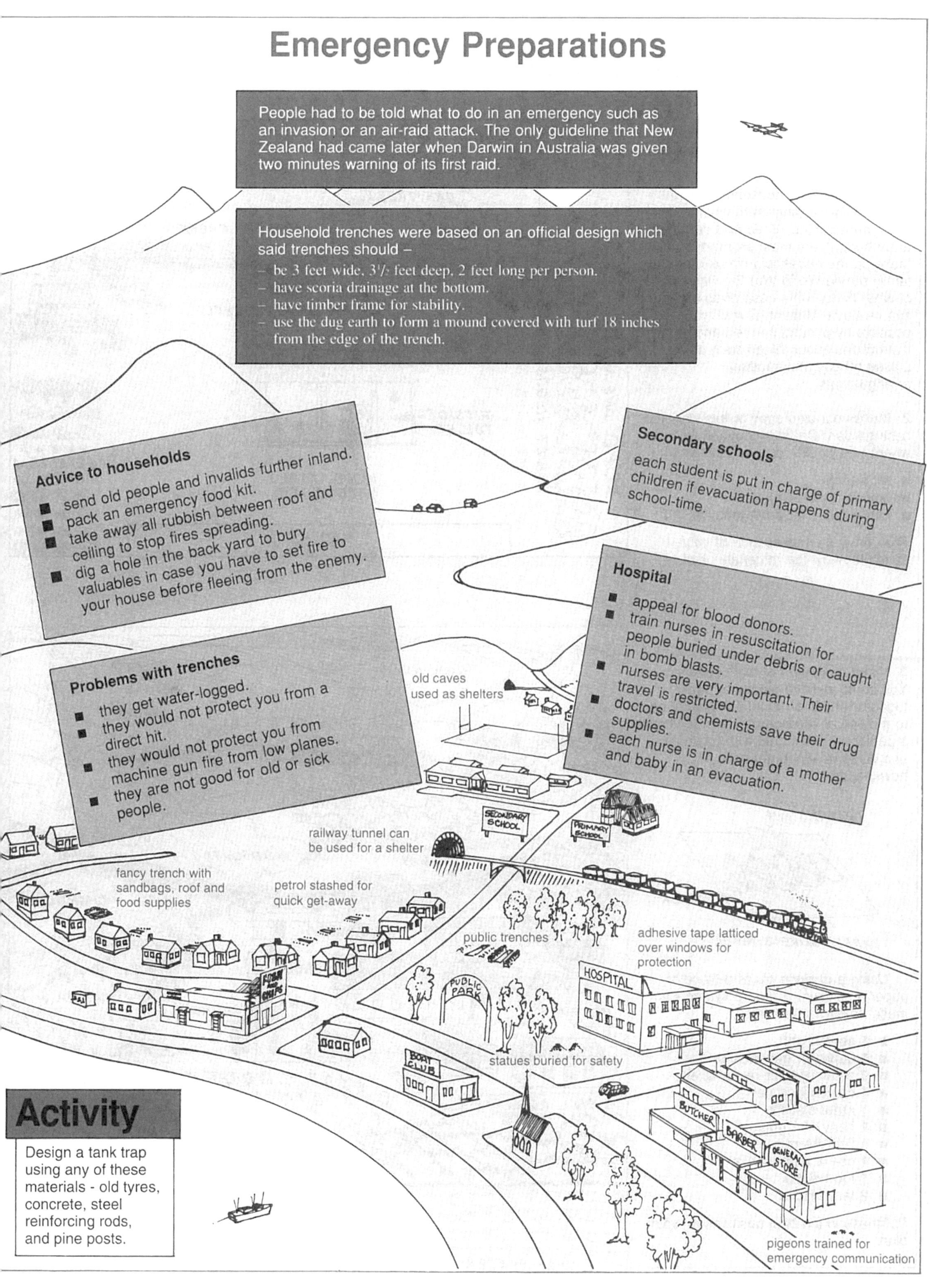
Emergency Preparations
People had to be told what to do in an emergency such as an invasion or an air-raid attack. The only guideline that New Zealand had came later when Darwin in Australia was given two minutes warning of its first raid.
Household trenches were based on an official design which said trenches should –
– be 3 feet wide, 3½ feet deep, 2 feet long per person.
– have scoria drainage at the bottom.
– have timber frame for stability.
– use the dug earth to form a mound covered with turf 18 inches from the edge of the trench.
Advice to households
■ send old people and invalids further inland.
■ pack an emergency food kit.
■ take away all rubbish between roof and ceiling to stop fires spreading.
■ dig a hole in the back yard to bury valuables in case you have to set fire to your house before fleeing from the enemy.
Secondary schools
each student is put in charge of primary children if evacuation happens during school-time.
Hospital
■ appeal for blood donors.
■ train nurses in resuscitation for people buried under debris or caught in bomb blasts.
■ nurses are very important. Their travel is restricted.
■ doctors and chemists save their drug supplies.
■ each nurse is in charge of a mother and baby in an evacuation.
Problems with trenches
■ they get water-logged.
■ they would not protect you from a direct hit.
■ they would not protect you from machine gun fire from low planes.
■ they are not good for old or sick people.
old caves used as shelters
railway tunnel can be used for a shelter
fancy trench with sandbags, roof and food supplies
petrol stashed for quick get-away
public trenches
adhesive tape latticed over windows for protection
statues buried for safety
pigeons trained for emergency communication
SECONDARY SCHOOL
PRIMARY SCHOOL
PUBLIC PARK
HOSPITAL
BOAT CLUB
BUTCHER
BARBER
GENERAL STORE
Activity
Design a tank trap using any of these materials - old tyres, concrete, steel reinforcing rods, and pine posts.

Activities

1 Find a copy of the Civil Defence policy for your area today. Note how it is set out. Make sure you understand what is required of you in the case of a disaster.

During the war, households were sent circulars, telling them what to do. They were printed in red and designed to be hung in the most prominent place. Make up the household circular for your family during World War 2 giving details of what to do in the case of an air and sea invasion. Make it as real as possible by printing it in red and giving instructions about things such as cutting off gas and sanitary arrangements.

2 Make your own copy of this war-time back garden. On your copy, show where you would put these things –

- slit trench
- hole for family treasures
- hiding place for emergency kit.

Then draw a cross-section of your trench to show the materials used.

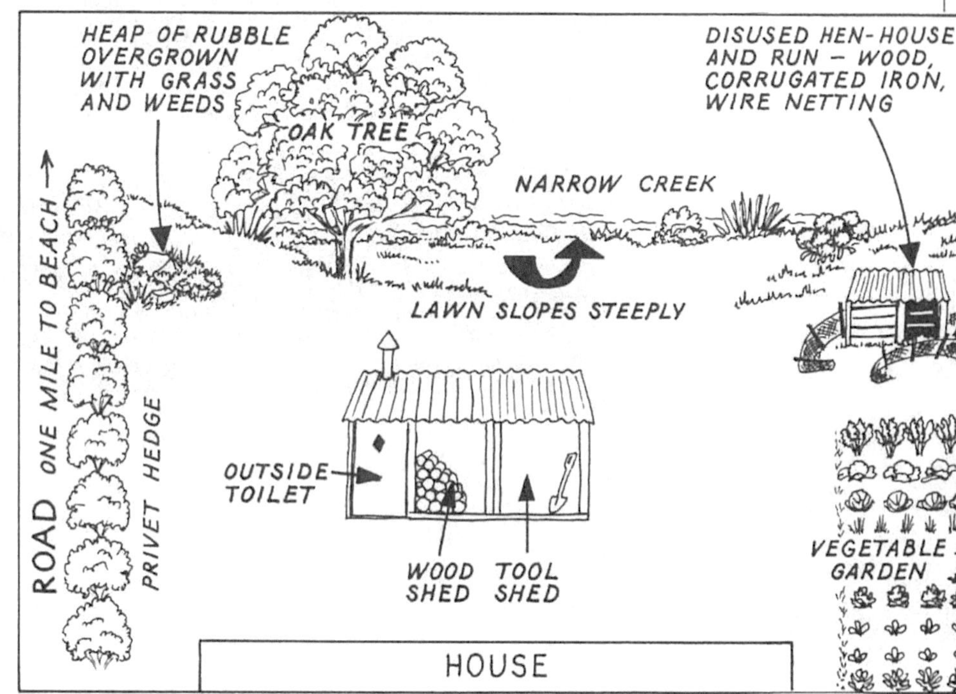

3 Make a big plan of this settlement. You could join two pieces of paper together and draw it out OR paint it on to a piece of cardboard or ply OR make a papier-mache model with paste (flour and water is adequate) and newspapers.

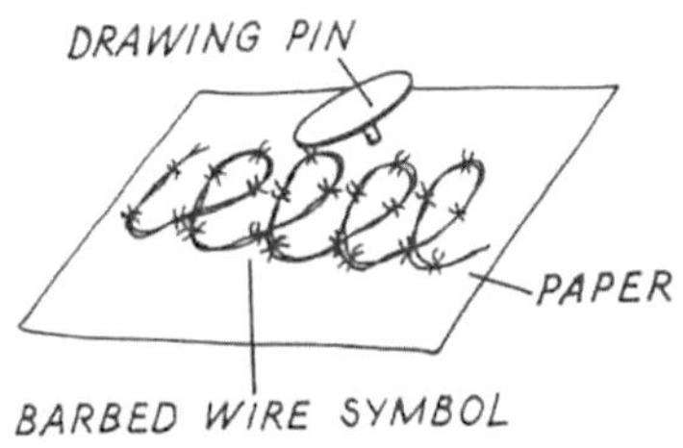

Using a drawing pin and piece of paper as shown, make up symbols for these defence measures.

- 1 searchlight
- 1 depot for gas masks
- 1 communal air-raid shelter
- 1 camouflage net
- 1 radar station
- 1 heavy AA gun
- 1 light AA gun
- 1 coil of barbed wire
- 1 food dump
- 2 tank blocks

Put these in the best positions on your plan.

Kia Matara – The Home Guard

The Home Guard was ready to defend New Zealand from invasion.

Kia Matara means *on guard* and was the motto for the New Zealand Home Guard, set up in August 1940.

It was compulsory for all men of military age not in the army and for men between 46 and 50. Exceptions were policemen, firemen, seamen, key members of the E.P.S. (Emergency Precautions Service), doctors, chemists, magistrates, judges, Ministers of religion, disabled, blind, those in hospital or prison. Although Maori men were also exempt, a lot of them joined the Home Guard. At one time, there were 124,000 Home Guardsmen.

To start with, they did not have uniforms or guns and so they wore an armband for identification and used wooden rifles for arms drill. During practices, they could use things like packets of flour as hand grenades and tin rattles to make machine gun sounds. The day they were at last issued with battle-dress and boots, tommy guns, heavy and light machine guns, Thompson sub machine guns, rounds of small arms ammunition and rifles was a very happy one for the Home Guardsmen.

Special Commando units spent a lot of time in the bush and hills where they had hide-outs with radio, ammunition, explosives and food supplies. During an enemy invasion, they were to go to their hide-outs and attack the enemy from the rear.

The Motor Transport Organisation was spread over New Zealand. It got ready to carry supplies, ammunition and petrol for the army in an emergency. Each full company had 79 three ton lorries, 4 cars, 8 motorcycles and 155 men. Petrol was stored and guarded all over the country.

The Engineering units learned skills such as trestle bridge building, using knots and lashings for nails, map and compass reading. The Signals units made lamps from camera tripods and reflectors from treacle tins. When they practised from hills at night, people became scared that spies were on the loose.

The Bomb Disposal Group had training at Trentham. They learned about enemy bombs and how to deal with enemy and British mines which came on to the West coasts of the North and South Islands and the Coromandel Peninsula and Bay of Islands.

The Home Guard was expected to...

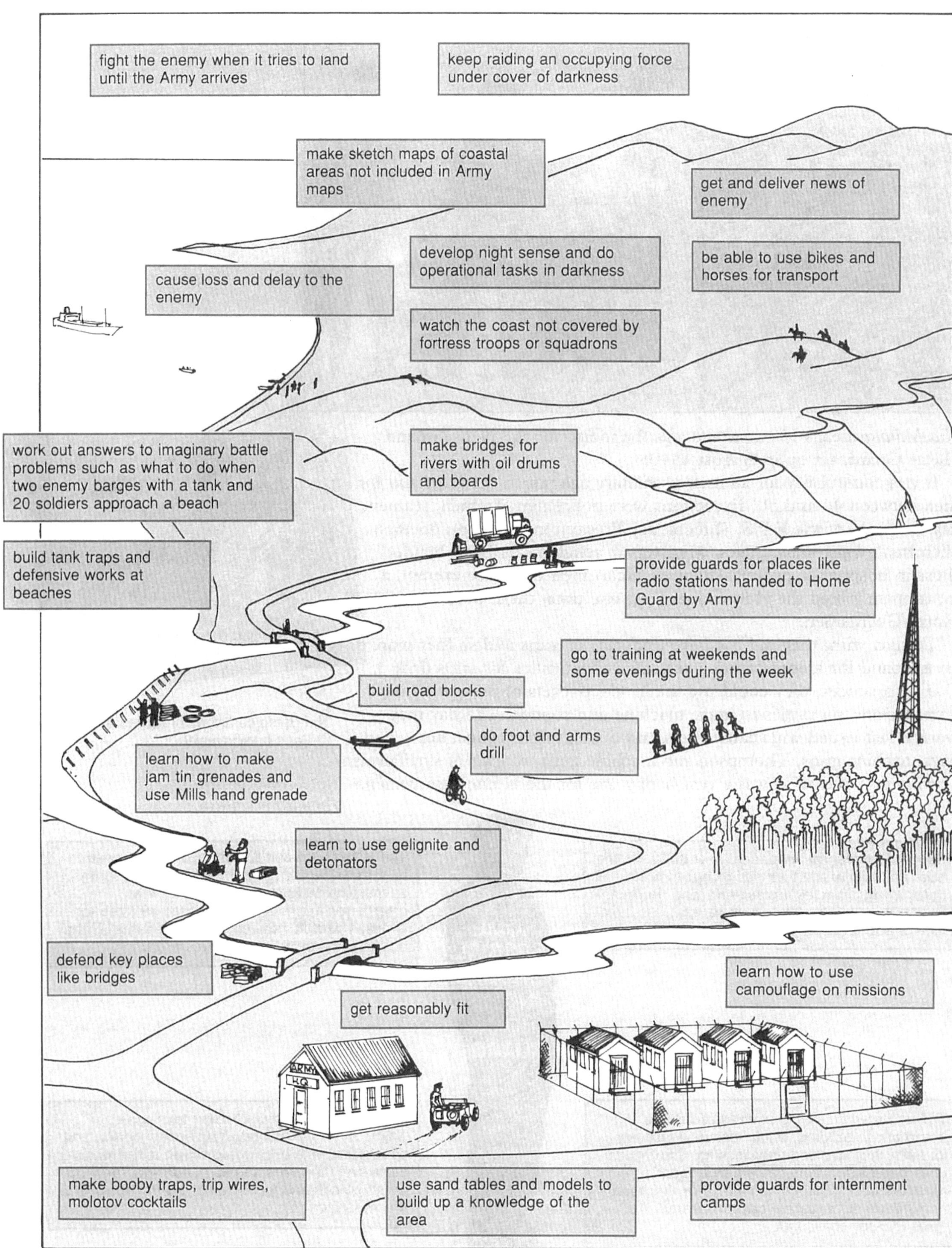

Activities

1 Use a full page to make your own drawing of the Home Guardsman and fill out the boxes. Make each box 5cms square.

2 Design these for your Home Guardsman.

- an armband
- a carving for his wooden rifle
- a badge
- his commando bush hide-out

3 Number 1–20 down your page. Beside each number, write words which fits the clues, using only letters from the boxes. All the words are from the unit on The Home Guard.

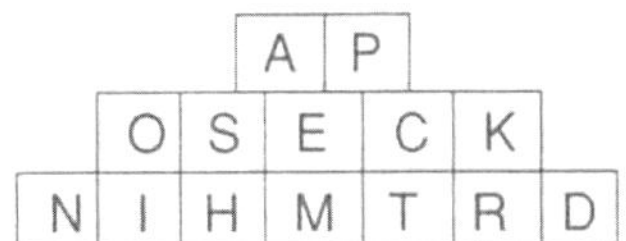

1. motto
2. exempt but joined
3. made of all areas (2 words)
4. identification worn here
5. gun type
6. transport
7. to slow enemy
8. had to be guarded
9. drifted ashore
10. used by signals (2 words)
11. training camp
12. special raider
13. excellent cover
14. caused by night signals
15. direction finder
16. used with gelignite
17. engineers used instead of nails
18. made good grenades
19. had to be blocked
20. watched at all times

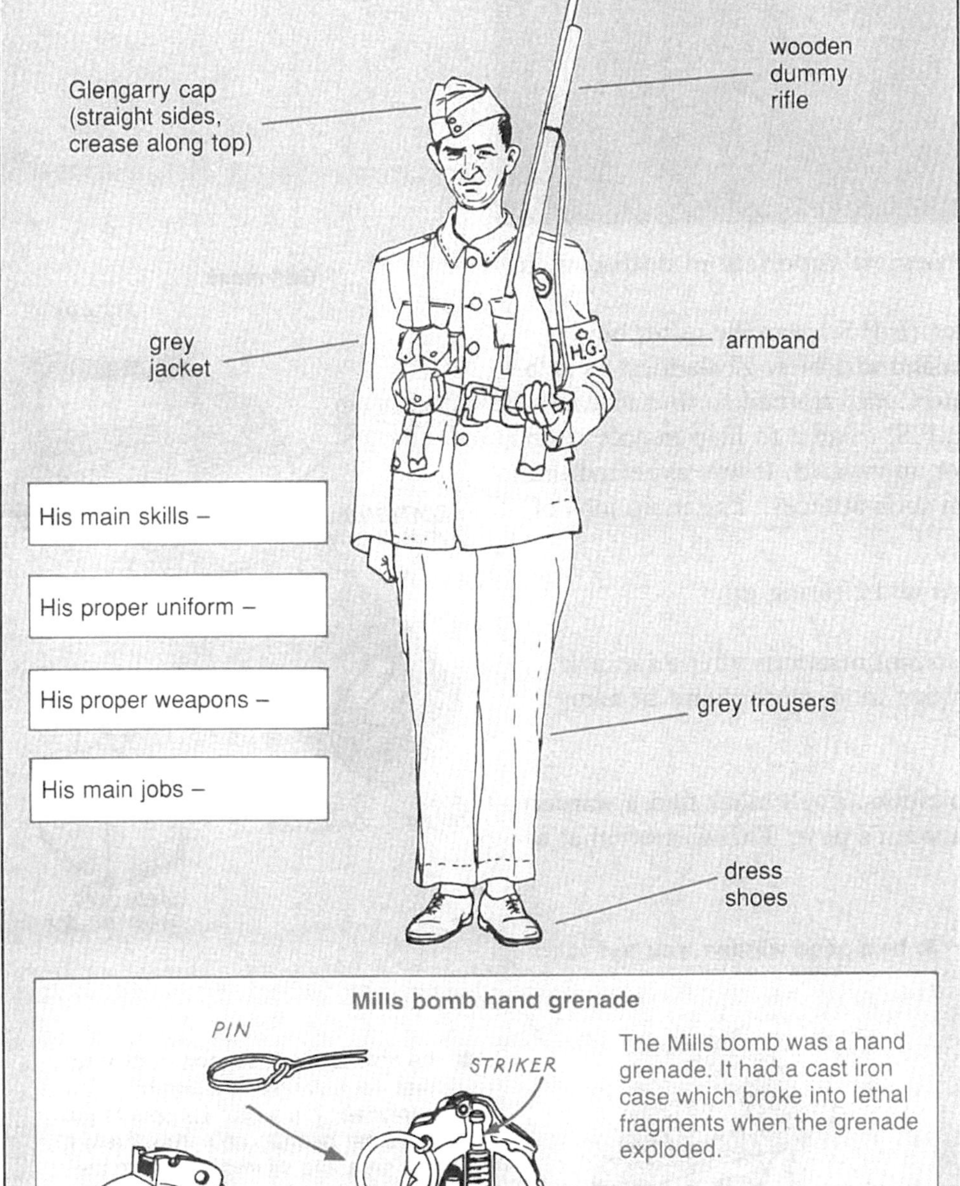

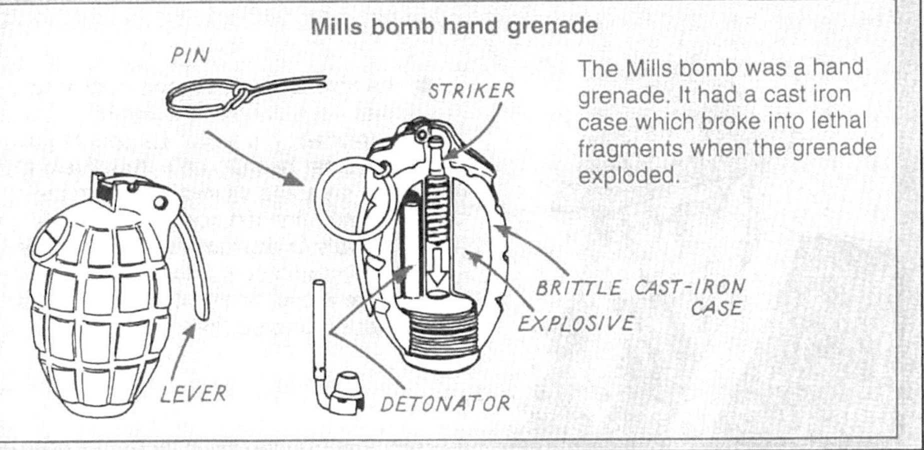

The Mills bomb was a hand grenade. It had a cast iron case which broke into lethal fragments when the grenade exploded.

4 With a friend, draw sketch maps to work out the best option for these problems used for Home Guard practice.

A Your Home Guard platoon is guarding a hydro electric dam when enemy soldiers appear at the far end of the slipway, having removed the sentries you had placed there. Their line of approach will very quickly bring them to the power house. You have a Thompson sub machine gun, 5 home-made rockets, 1 light mortar.

B A mine has drifted onto the beach during a fierce storm. It is very near the primary school.

C You have five Home Guardsmen with you when you see an enemy scouting platoon is approaching crossroads which are most important to a defensive supply route. You have one Bren gun, three Mills bombs grenades, five molotov cocktails.

5 When the Army took over the Home Guard in 1941, commissions were then granted. Nominate your partner for one, giving a reason. You could arrange a ceremony.

People for crisis – The E.P.S.

It was thought that while ordinary citizens would have time to escape from the gas, people like the E.P.S. would need gas mask

Everybody realised that team work was most important in dealing with an emergency.

The Emergency Precautions Service (E.P.S.) was the other big organisation set up to make New Zealand and New Zealanders as safe as possible during the war. The Home Guard trained so that it would be ready to fight the enemy, while the E.P.S. trained to help people after a hit and run bombardment from sea or an air-raid. It was expected that people and property would be hurt in such atttacks. The main jobs of the E.P.S. would be –

- fighting fires from bomb explosions and clearing up
- dealing with gas attacks
- controlling water, electricity and communications after an attack
- helping people in shock and supplying food, clothes and bedding
- dealing with unexploded bombs

On maps, towns were divided into blocks. Each block had a warden and a deputy warden and a special warden's post. This was often at a school.

Gas mask

STRAPS
CELLULOID WINDOW
BREATHING VALVE
AIR INLET
FILTER CANISTER
CARDBOARD CARRYING BOX

To be a good warden, you had to ...

- have a detailed knowledge of the streets and people.
- know which houses had telephones that could be used in an emergency.
- have plans so that if telephones were out of action, messages could be sent by car, motor cycle, bike or runners. Boy scouts made good runners.
- know exactly where all the water mains and fire hydrants were.

- be able to make reports quickly so that, for example, if a bomb exploded, you would be able to get stretcher bearers and fire-fighters to the area and injured people to the nearest first aid post.
- be able to deal with tricky situations like making sure unexploded bombs were roped off and damaged shops were protected from looting.

The bomb that frightened New Zealanders was called a fire bomb or an incendiary bomb. These bombs caused terrible damage to London. They had a filling that burned very easily and a special magnesium case which melted and sent out very fierce flares. They started fires which could very quickly get out of control.

Everybody was worried about fires especially as many of New Zealand's buildings were wooden. It was very important to prevent fires because the war had stopped materials being available for re-building. People were told to keep tubs and buckets full of water, and to put a thin film of oil on top to stop sandflies.

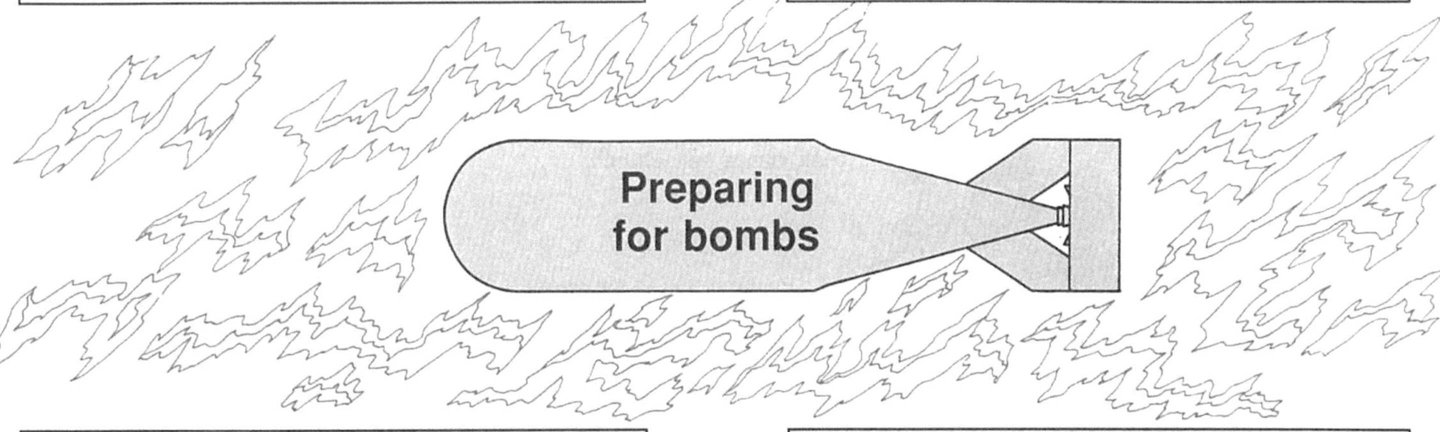

Preparing for bombs

Business premises were told to have 44 gallon drums on each floor with buckets close by. City Councils provided dry sand cheaply. In 1941 the Government passed special regulations about the fire bombs. It said that people who owned buildings must –

- provide two 20 pound bags of sand for each floor and a bucket pump with a hose and spray nozzle.
- have fire guards, three men per bucket pump, living within 15 minutes of the building, ready to leave at once when the alarm went.
- have at least one person on fire watching duty.

The general public were given lessons on dealing with incendiary bombs. Some of the methods taught were

- smother the bomb in sand
- douse the bomb with a fine spray of water
- throw buckets of water over it
- dunk the bomb rapidly in a large bucket of water.

Fire duty was compulsory for all male staff who were not in the Home Guard or the E.P.S. If a man refused, he could get a fine of up to £50 or three months in prison. Women did a lot of fire watching too.

Activities

1 In your notebook, rearrange these three columns into the correct order.

The first one is done for you.

1 air	raid	bomb attack
2 bucket	....*.....	........*.........
3 ....*.....	....*.....	........*.........

Column 1	Column 2	Column 3
1 air	bomb	anti-fire gear
2 bucket	bomb	bomb attack
3 celluloid	duty	breathing apparatus
4 deputy	hydrant	helps chief
5 fire	main	much feared
6 fire	mask	necessary in crisis
7 fire	pump	part of mask
8 gas	raid	piped supply
9 team	warden	possible dud
10 unexploded	windows	water outlet
11 water	work	watching

2 Warden Assessment
You are the warden of a real or imaginary area in 1941.

A Draw a map of your area showing any –

- key targets such as airfields, wharves, long bridges, industrial plant
- schools
- private and/or public hospitals
- sports fields or race tracks
- factory complexes such as dairy factory, freezing works
- council chamber, Town Hall, church

B Mark in the best places for 5 First Aid Posts, 2 Advanced Dressing Stations (for severe wounds) and your office.

C Give everyone in the class or group a job to do in the event of an emergency.

D Write a few sentences saying where you would expect the main problem areas to be that you would need to keep a careful eye on.

3 Fire fighting can be very dangerous. Find out about modern methods and equipment used in training nowadays. You might be able to get your local brigade to talk to you.

Women's response

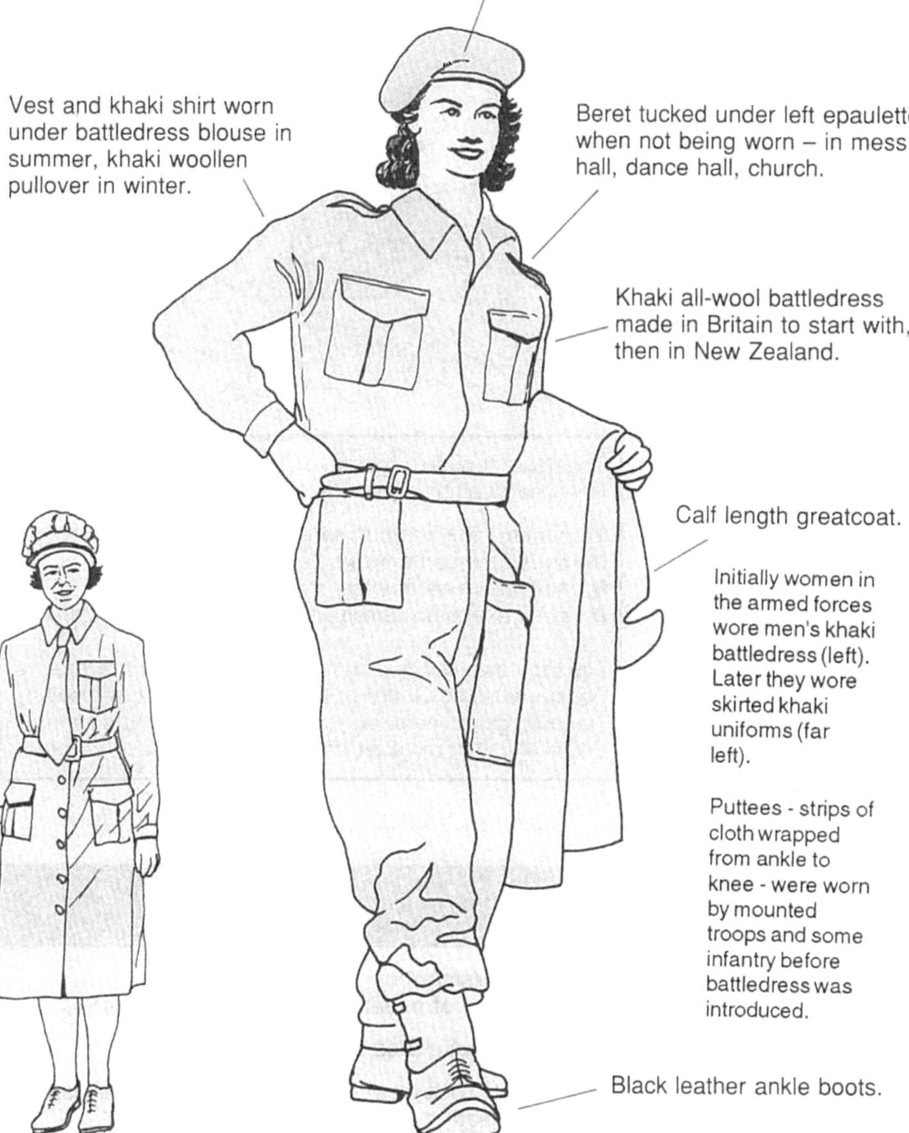

Initially women in the armed forces wore men's khaki battledress (left). Later they wore skirted khaki uniforms (far left).

Puttees - strips of cloth wrapped from ankle to knee - were worn by mounted troops and some infantry before battledress was introduced.

The special badge of the Women's War Service Auxiliary. Officers had the same badge with the word 'OFFICIAL' on a scroll underneath.

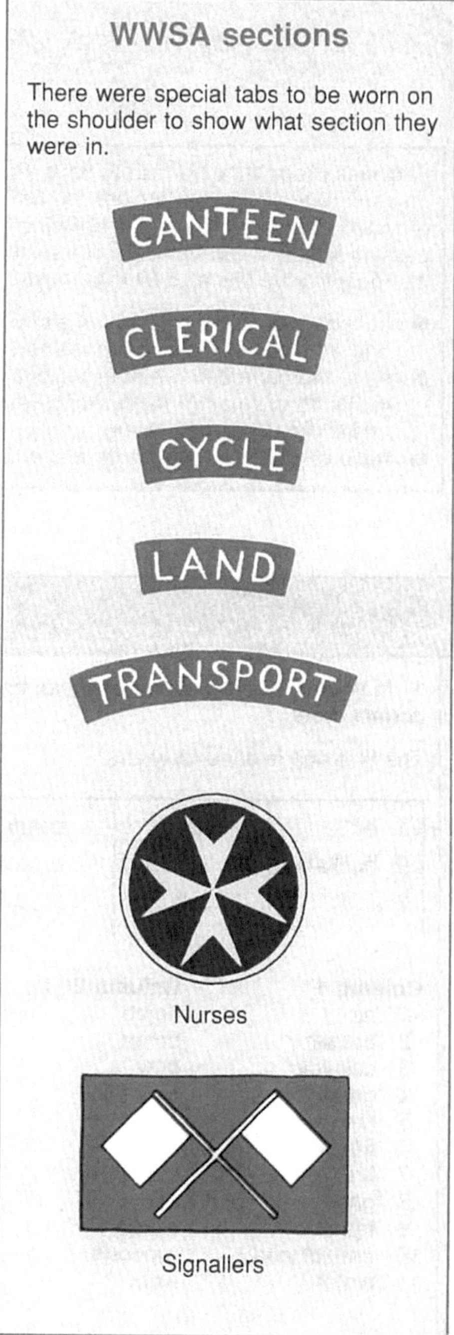

WWSA sections

There were special tabs to be worn on the shoulder to show what section they were in.

Nurses

Signallers

The third special organisation set up to defend New Zealand was the Women's War Service Auxiliary. Its members often worked with the Home Guard and some went overseas to work in New Zealand forces clubs where they were called 'Tuis'.

Each member paid £1 for the uniform. Their uniform was a long-sleeved belted dress of khaki cotton drill with buttons up the front and three large military style pockets and a soft crowned visored khaki cap, badge and tie.

When they were not in uniform, they wore an armband with a Crown and the W.W.S.A in red on white cloth.

New Zealanders quickly got used to seeing large numbers of women and men in uniform. To start with, women were given the men's khaki battledress and only later got the women's skirted khaki uniform.

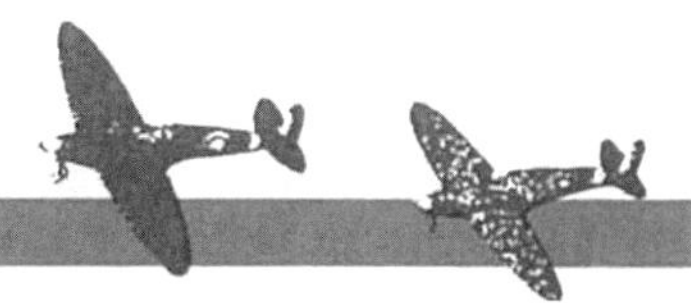

At the beginning of the war, women were expected to stay at home and support the men who would do the fighting and working in factories for the war effort. Magazines and newspapers told them that now, more than ever, they should dress and behave in as pretty a way as possible to make men feel better. When some women offered to fill the gaps left by men in jobs, they were told it was a terrible idea.

But more and more New Zealand men were going overseas to fight and the only way to keep factories and land producing was to have women working there. The idea was that this would be just for the war and when it ended, women would go back to their right place, in the home. And all through the war, there was the belief that women with children under 16 should not be asked to work and should instead stay home to look after their children. There was hardly anywhere for mothers to leave children anyway.

It was not only men who joined the Services to fight Hitler. Women also joined all branches of the Services as –

- WAACs (Women's Army Auxiliary Corps)
- WAAFs (Women's Auxiliary Air Force)
- WRENs (Women's Royal Naval Service)

Activities

1 Play the **WAR WORKING WOMEN'S SKILLS GAME** in your group or with a partner. You will need a dice.

When there was something that people during the war needed but did not have, they made it. You can make your own dice out of thick paper or card and sellotape by ruling squares with the numbers written in, cutting the shape out and folding it. You could fill it with sand to make it heavy.

Take turns to roll dice. If you roll a **1**, you collect a skill worth 1 mark anywhere in the first column. If you roll a **2**, collect a skill worth 2 marks from that column and so on.

Make a note of the number of the skill you collect each time because it can only be collected once.

When you have finished write out all the skills you have collected, explain what they are and then total their value. The winner is the one with the highest score.

2 Make your own drawing of a New Zealand service woman or man in their uniform.

3 A lot of people were trained in Morse Code during the war. It could be sent in a number of different ways – flashing a light, waving a flag, making sounds, even blinking your eyes or using the sun.

A . _	B _ . . .	C _ . _ .
D _ . .	E .	F . . _ .
G _ _ .	H	I . .
J . _ _ _	K _ . _	L . _ . .
M _ _	N _ .	O _ _ _
P . _ _ .	Q _ _ . _	R . _ .
S . . .	T _	U . . _
V . . . _	W . _ _	X _ . . _
Y _ . _ _	Z _ _ . .	

Use the code to send some signals to your partner.

4 Oral History. Questionnaire and/or interview.
Prepare a questionnaire under the general heading of '*Organisations and measures set up to defend New Zealand during World War 2*'.

WAR WORKING WOMEN'S SKILLS GAME

column 1	column 2	column 3	column 4	column 5	column 6
1/ lathe work	2/ crane driving	3/ morse coding	4/ police work	5/ traffic control	6/ bomb disposing
7/ lorry driving	8/ despatch riding	9/ tramline repairing	10/ map reading	11/ parachute packing	12/ herd testing
13/ search light operating	14/ post delivering	15/ bus driving	16/ ambulance driving	17/ train station duties	18/ mechanic work
19/ train conducting	20/ taxi driving	21/ radar operations	22/ wireless operations	23/ truck driving	24/ plane wing mending
25/ medical orderly	26/ wing cover making	27/ canteen working	28/ Army cooking	29/ telegraphing	30/ meteoro-logical work
31/ map plotting	32/ machine coding	33/ route marching	34/ first aid	35/ air-raid safety	36/ plane instrument maintenance
37/ night riding	38/ engineer work	39/ fire watching	40/ photography	41/ fire fighting	42/ fitness instructing
43/ telephone operating	44/ train van cleaning	45/ mail delivery	46/ tram conducting	47/ club work	48/ safety gear maintenance
49/ milk delivery	50/ gas warfare precautions	51/ gunnery research	52/ high explosives precautions	53/ bomber instructing	54/ Govt. market gardening work
55/ weapon shooting	56/ AA gun work	57/ train guard assisting	58/ office work	59/ farm work	60/ weapon making
61/ VAD (Voluntary Aid Detachment)	62/ night class study	63/ work overseas	64/ work on hospital ships	65/ work with the H.G. and E.P.S.	66/ Red Cross transport driver

There will be people in your community who were either themselves members of the special groups such as the Services, Home Guard, E.P.S., WWSA, or know people who were. Many of them will have interesting stories to tell you. It might be possible to find someone who is willing to be interviewed.

War-time entertainment

Country

A & P Shows
Women's Institutes and Division of Farmers' Union.

Dances

Formal such as Deb Ball or Military Ball. Informal such as woolshed dance. Dances were waltzes, fox trots, two steps. The most bold dance was jitter bugging (a bit like rock and roll) but this was often banned because it was too wild.

Songs

We'll Meet Again
When They Sound the Last All-Clear
There'll Always Be An England
Coming In On a Wing and a Prayer
When the Lights Go On Again All Over the World
Kiss Me Goodnight, Sergeant Major
Roll Out the Barrel
Boots And All
The Kiwis On Parade
Freedom's Army
The NZ Boys Are Marching
Maori Battalion Marching Song

Gardening

DIG FOR VICTORY

Pioneering habit of building a house and planting a garden round it, flower in front and vegetable at back. During war-time, gardens became even more important.

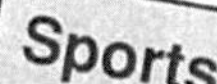

Sports

Rugby (Ranfurly Shield Match played in August 1939, next one was not till 1946).
Golf
Tennis
Tramping
Shooting
Yachting
Swimming

Hops

Informal dances without chaperones were called 'hops'.

Churches

Important social centres. Mothers' Unions and Women's Guilds.

Movies

The movies cost 1s 6d (15c). People like nurses got in for 1s (10c). Some of the hit movies were:
Hitler, Beast of Berlin
Goodbye Mr Chips
Gone With the Wind
Wuthering Heights
Laddie
Son of Monte Cristo
The Invisible Woman
Pride and Prejudice

Cards

Many dances were combined with a card evening, usually euchre. Mothers chaperoned daughters and played cards.

Kiwi Concert Party

Entertained troops overseas but made quick tour of New Zealand in 1943 to raise money for the Patriotic Fund.

Newsreels

Citizen Soldiers (Home Guard training)
The Hurry Up Squad (Army crash courses)
Warden's Post (Air raid precautions)

Centennial Exhibition 1940 – Rongotai, Wellington

Huge displays featuring New Zealand geography, history and life-styles. Included a vast amusement park.

Activities

1 There were a lot of arguments for and against holding the 1940 Centennial Exhibition. Some people said the money should be spent on bombs and guns instead. Others said it would be a much needed tonic.
Write a letter to the newspaper, putting forward your opinion.

2 Plan out a New Zealand Exhibition for next year. Use a full page for this.

3 It is 1940. A friend, whose father has been killed in the war, is coming to stay for a week. Plan out an itinerary.

Radio

BBC programmes became part of New Zealand's way of life in war-time. Most important were Winston Churchill's speeches and meetings of the Brains Trust (arguments over moral issues).

Picnics

Going to picnics on bikes was popular.

Your light is showing!

After a while, New Zealanders got over their fear of German bombers. New Zealand was a long way from the fighting. But when Japan came into the war, fears about being bombed, came back. The Aichi D3A2, for example, had a range of 970 miles and the Nakajima B5N2 had a range of 1400 miles.

It was decided New Zealand needed blacking out to stay safe.

Some black-out rules

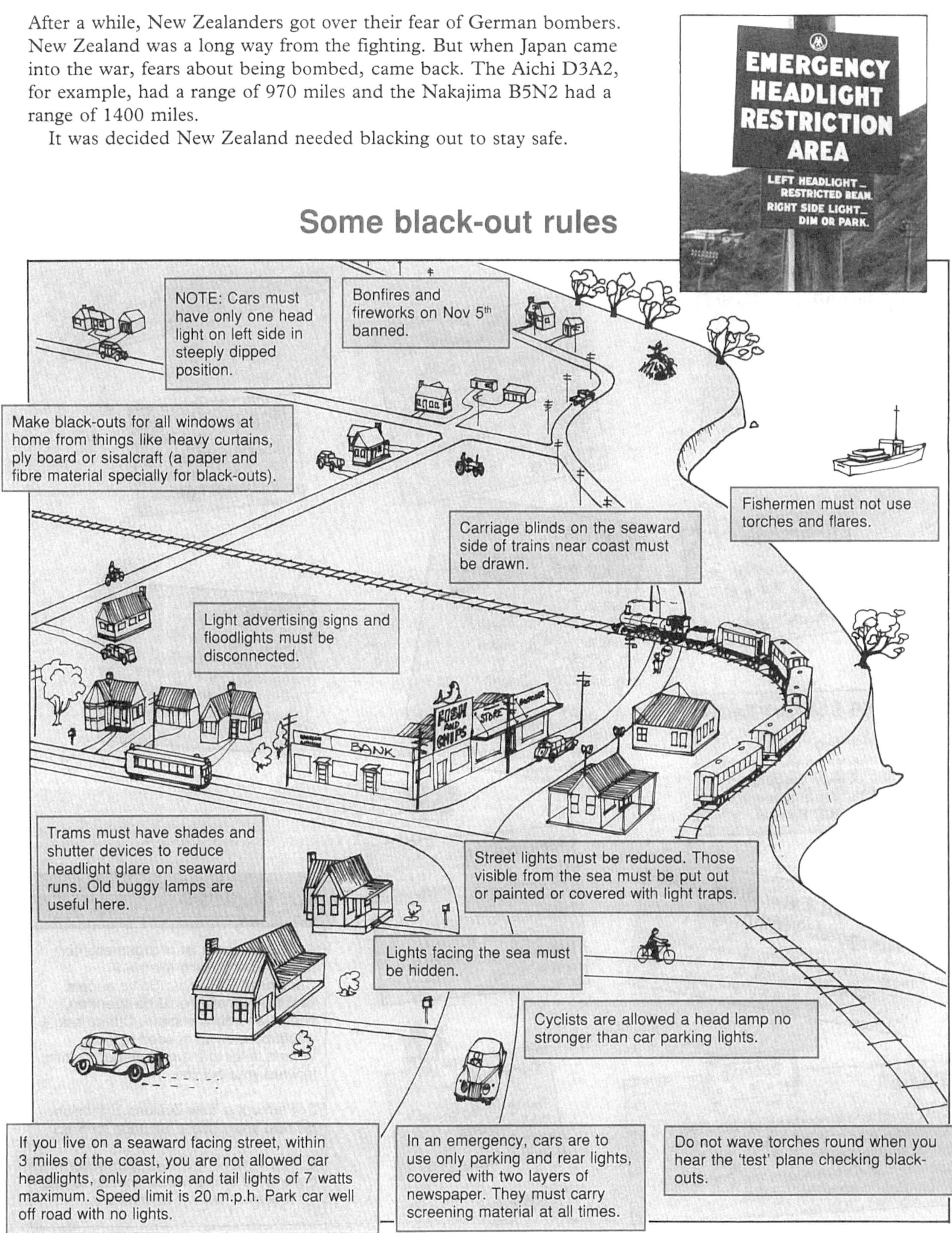

A visit from the warden

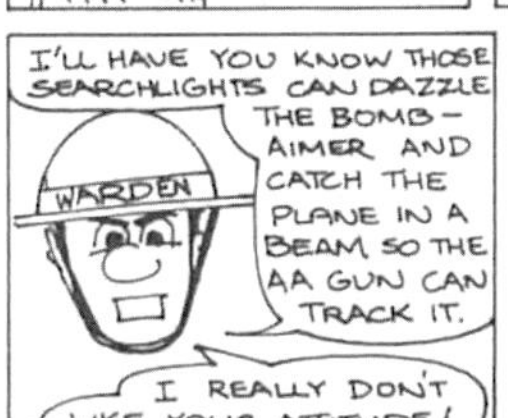

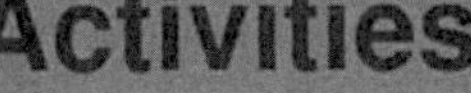

Activities

1 Some war-time people

- tram driver
- farmer
- widow
- night class tutor
- hotel owner
- nurse
- fisherman
- theatre owner
- policeman
- night factory worker
- taxi driver
- wharfie
- 'test' pilot
- baker
- Army cook
- thief
- searchlight crewman
- courting man or woman
- owner of hardware shop
- five year old
- night cartman
- candle maker
- train driver
- boarding school pupil
- warden
- astronomer
- church minister
- prison warden
- ambulance driver
- drapery shop owner

Everyone in your class or group becomes one of the above. Your teacher or group leader will keep a list. Work out one sentence about what you must do during the black-out that will be a fair clue for the others to guess who you are. A warden, for example, might say, '*It is a heavy responsibility and I find some people abusive when I point out the errors of their ways*'.

Walk round the class, having small conversations. Ask each other what you think of the black-out regulations. Beside the name of each person, write down what job you think they have.

The teacher or group leader will read out the list to see who got the most right.

2 At 9 o'clock at night in June 1942, Doctor Waikato has to leave her house to attend an emergency at the Clancy home, 20 kilometres away. Imagine you are Doctor Waikato. Describe your car journey.

3

N.	E.	S.	W.

Rule up the four squares as shown which represent the north, east, south, west walls of your home. If you have more than one storey, add them to the top. Make your squares 5 cms x 5 cms. Using only war-time materials and trying to keep within a limited budget, show a blackout plan.

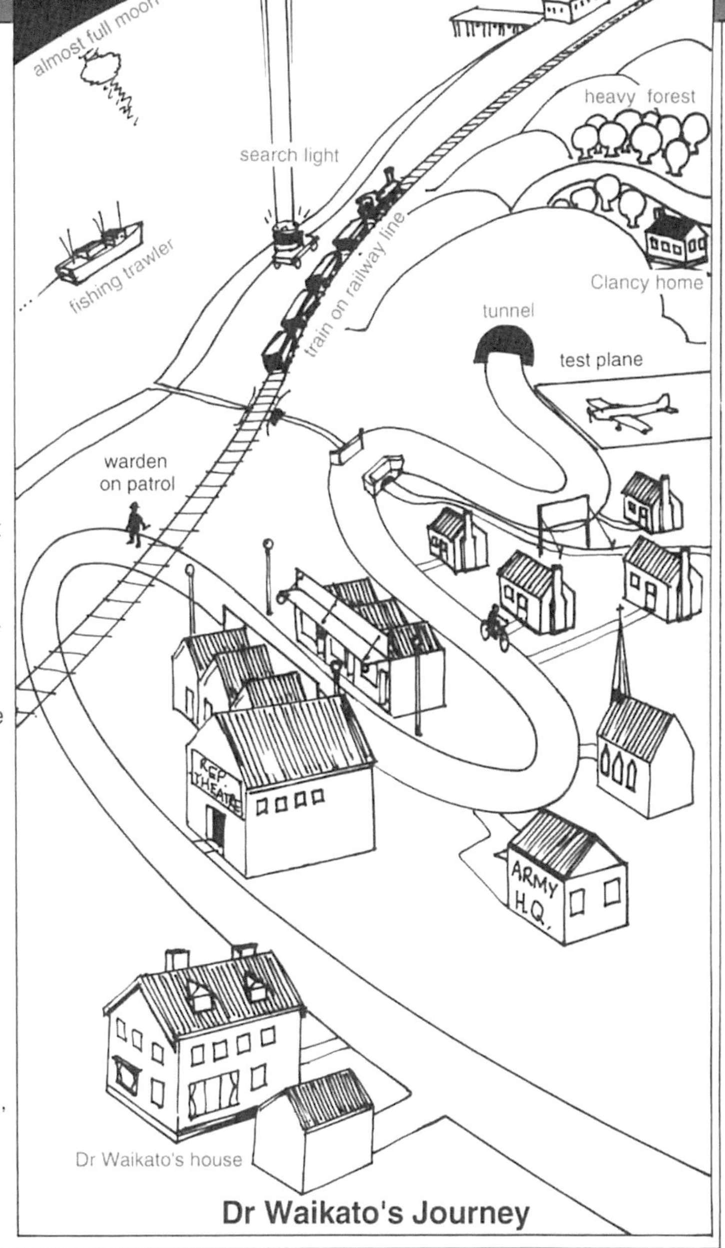

Dr Waikato's Journey

Being a good patriot

Patriotic means caring about your country. Thousands and thousands of New Zealanders, including children, worked very hard for their country during the war. They gave up many hours of spare time. All this was voluntary work. One of the most important things they did was to collect and make articles which they packed into parcels.

PARCELS

home comforts packed in parcels and sent to ...

Prisoner of War Camps
Many New Zealanders were held in P.O.W. camps. Parcels were sent to the camps by the Red Cross.

New Zealand service people overseas
The desert, for example, could be freezing at night. Newspapers and magazines from New Zealand would make him feel closer to home.

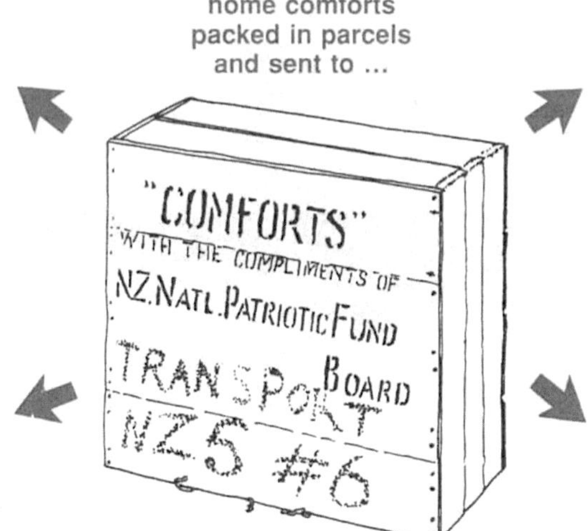

Britain
People in Britain were having a much worse time of the war than New Zealanders.

Training Camps
As well as soldiers, thousands of people like pilots, aircrew, mechanics and wireless operators, were training in New Zealand.

The organisation that was set up to be responsible for this overall welfare of the forces was called **'The National Patriotic Fund'**.

The prisoner of war parcels from the Red Cross were very important in helping the prisoners know they had not been forgotten. The aim was one parcel per man per week. The Red Cross Society voluntary workers packed parcels at a speed of seven a minute. Each Red Cross parcel weighed 11 pounds (nearly 5 kg). It contained tins of cheese, jam, coffee and milk powder, honey or condensed milk, tins of meat, sultanas, dried peas, chocolate, butter, sugar and tea.

When people were packing their own parcels for sending overseas, they had to be careful to use special recipes that did away with ingredients such as nuts and milk which send cakes mouldy.

These were the main recommended items for parcels -

home made cakes	ginger nuts	shortbread
soap	razor blades	writing materials
bootlaces	handkerchiefs	cakes of chocolate
tins of sweets	plain postcards	tins of fruit salts
sea boot stockings	heel-less socks	balaclavas
gloves	mittens	pullovers
buttons	tins of meat	cigarettes
tins of fruit	footpowder	playing cards
small books	tins of coffee	milk powder

Parcel day was very important to the people overseas so everyone in New Zealand tried to help. If they knew of someone who was packing a parcel for overseas, they would try to bring a contribution.

49 Hautana St
25th March/43 Lower Hutt
Hello, hello, you soldier boy. Hope you are fit & well & going strong. I am sending these biscuits just as a little appreciation for what you are doing for us all. Only sorry the tin is so small. I hope it will not be long before you are turning homewards again. Cheerio! & often the c-c-p-w. from Mrs W. H. Smith.

Sometimes a little note from a complete stranger was slipped into the parcel. This is one that a soldier overseas received in 1943.

Other ways of helping the war effort

Students used coins to make 'copper trails.'

Tonnes and tonnes of clothing was sent from New Zealand to Britain during the war. The idea started when women and children in Britain lost their homes when the Germans bombed them. Old clothes were collected and sorted. Dry cleaning firms and transport firms worked free of charge. The women mended the clothes or used them to make new ones.

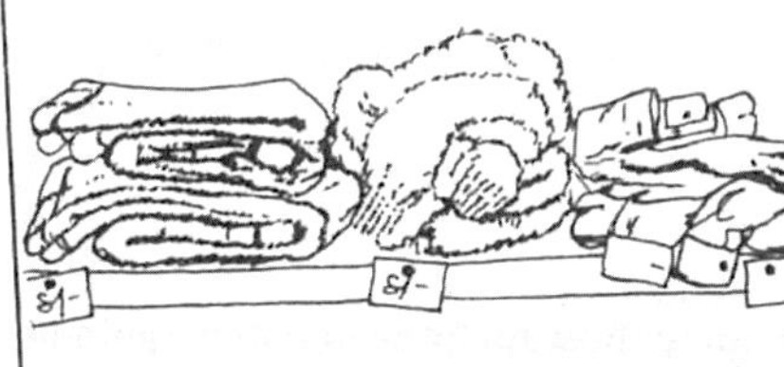

Farmers would give whole paddocks of a crop such as peas or potatoes to the Red Cross who would be able to sell these for patriotic funds.

Schools and churches raised money for the Patriotic Fund by putting on entertainments and doing odd jobs and growing vegetables to sell.

Country Women's Institute groups boiled down beasts to get the fat. This was sealed into tins and sent to England.

Special knitting groups were formed. A certain time at school might be set aside for this each week. Women and schoolgirls knitted socks, gloves, mittens, skull caps, balaclavas, scarves, jerseys and sea boot stockings. Boys sometimes knitted as well. Ordinary processed knitting wool soon became in short supply so women learnt how to spin and weave natural wools.

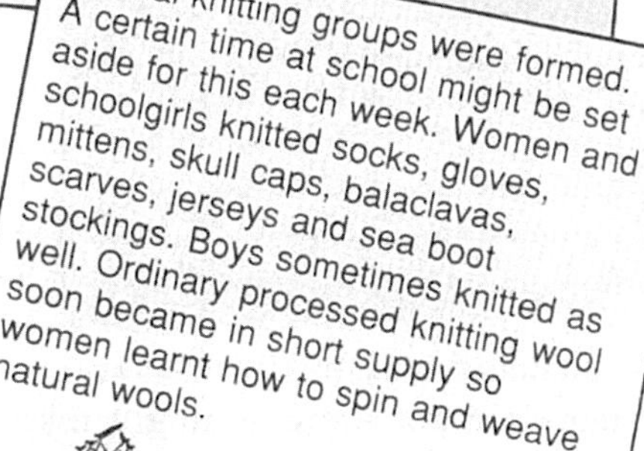

Spectators at football matches might be charged 6d entrance fee. This would be used for a special cause such as wounded soldiers.

The war was very expensive. New Zealanders were asked to finance the war by giving interest-free loans to the Government. Donors were mentioned in the newspapers. Millions of pounds were raised.

Special sewing groups were set up. As well as materials such as bandages, pyjamas and quilts for hospitals and First Aid posts, they made things like face cloths, hussifs and handkerchiefs for troops overseas.

This is the hussif given to a New Zealand pilot who trained in Canada. He was killed in the Battle of Britain.

Rolls up to a very small, neat roll.

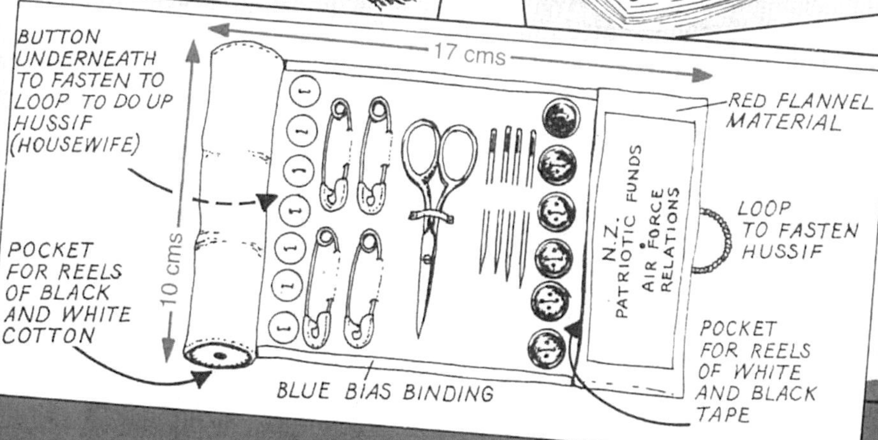

Activities

1 Hussifs were usually hand sewn. Make one of your own.

2 Design a poster for the New Zealand Patriotic Fund.

3 If you were to pack a parcel for overseas today list 12 items you would put in it.

4 Find out what sort of voluntary organisations operate in your district today. You may be able to pack a parcel to send overseas through an organisation like the Red Cross or Amnesty International.

5 A lot of New Zealanders remember the war as being a time of cooperation and team work. There was a feeling of working together for a common goal. Making sure everyone in your group takes part, make up some role plays of war-time situations. You may be able to put them on film.

- Prisoners of War waiting for parcel delivery.
- An inexperienced woman packing all the wrong things for her husband's parcel in front of her mother-in-law and friends.
- A knitting group in action.
- The Post Office dealing with badly wrapped parcels.
- Soldiers overseas reading notes in parcels from strangers in New Zealand.

The enemy wants information

When you joined the New Zealand Army during the war, you were given a small hard covered soldier's pay-book. Inside was a serious warning about always being on guard against the enemy. This is what it said –

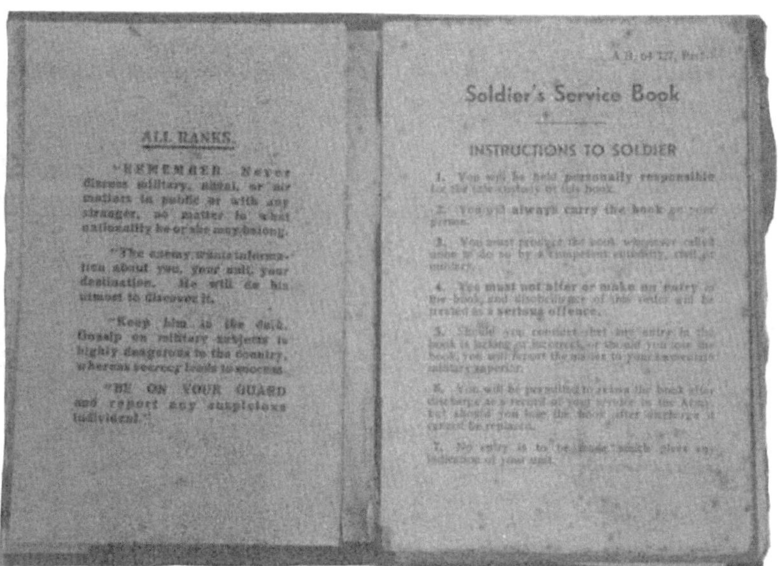

ALL RANKS.

"REMEMBER. Never discuss military, naval, or air matters in public or with any stranger, no matter to what nationality he or she may belong.

"The enemy wants information about you, your unit, your destination. He will do his utmost to discover it.

"Keep him in the dark. Gossip on military subjects is highly dangerous to the country, whereas secrecy leads to success.

"BE ON YOUR GUARD and report any suspicious individual."

A.B. 64 [illegible]

Soldier's Service Book

INSTRUCTIONS TO SOLDIER

1. You will be held personally responsible for the safe custody of this book.

2. You will always carry the book on your person.

3. You must produce the book whenever called upon to do so by a competent authority, civil or military.

4. You must not alter or make an entry in the book, and disobedience of this order will be treated as a serious offence.

5. Should you consider that any entry in the book is lacking or incorrect, or should you lose the book, you will report the matter to your immediate military superior.

6. You will be permitted to retain the book after discharge as a record of your service in the Army, but should you lose the book after discharge it cannot be replaced.

7. No entry is to be made which gives any indication of your unit.

It was very hard for women in New Zealand and men overseas, waiting eagerly for mail. The letters might not get there or might take months and months. When they did arrive, the censorship might have made them very hard to read. They might have blue pencil lines through them or even bits cut out. Sometimes only a photograph of the letter might arrive – not even the same size as the original.

If you had a friend or relative in a country such as Hungary that had been captured by the enemy, you could send a message to them through the Red Cross. You were not allowed to write more than 25 words.

This letter was sent to New Zealand from Hungary in 1943. At that time Hungary was occupied by Germany, New Zealand's enemy, and the letter had to be sent through the International Red Cross.

MAGYAR VÖRÖS-KERESZT
UNGARISCHES ROTES KREUZ
CROIX-ROUGE HONGROISE
BUDAPEST, VIII. BAROSS-UTCA 15. HONGRIE

Demandeur — Érdeklődő — Anfragesteller

Destinataire — Címzett — Empfänger

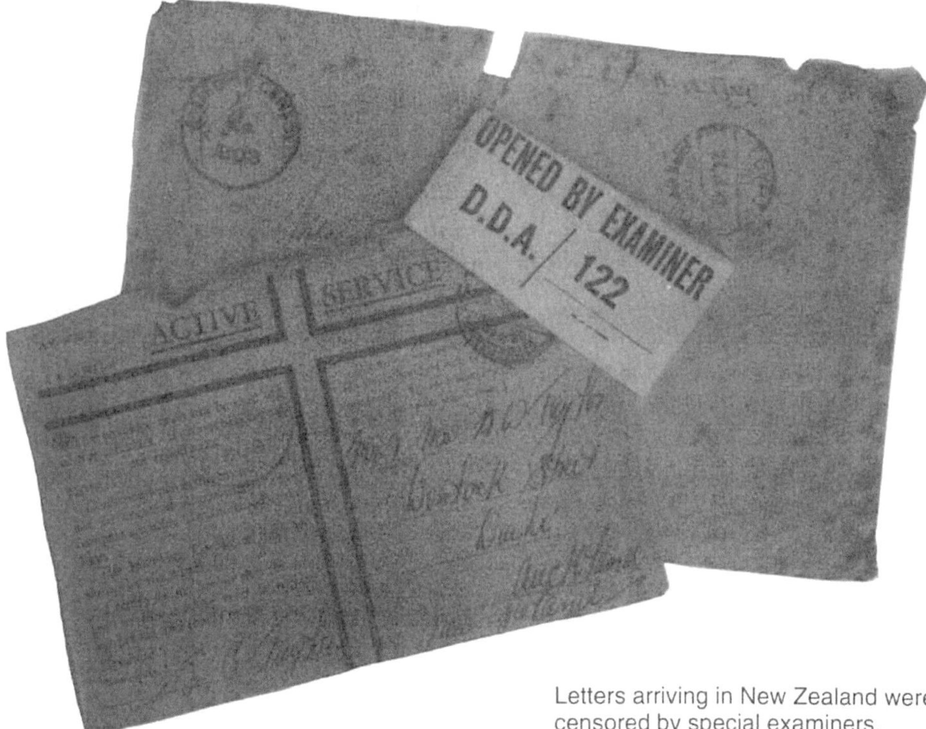

Letters arriving in New Zealand were censored by special examiners.

Ssh! Keep it under your hat – the enemy might be listening

ssh

New Zealand's censorship laws were very tight. The press especially complained that New Zealand was the most censor ridden country of the war. They could not understand, for example, why when trench digging started in Auckland's Albert Park, they were not allowed to say where it was happening. Yet the diggers must have known where they were digging and it was done during the day.

The man who had the final say about what news readers were allowed to say over the radio, which articles could be published in newspapers, journals or magazines, what could be filmed or listened to in public places, was Mr J. Paul. He was the Chief Censor in New Zealand during the war. Some people said he was the most powerful man in the country after the Prime Minister.

Letters were censored during the war. Letters written in a foreign language were sent to a special section in Wellington to be censored. During the war, they received letters in 44 different languages to deal with. It was impossible to keep in touch with overseas penfriends during the war. Very few such letters passed the censor, even to allied countries, in case they were really to enemy agents. All airmail was opened. Letters to servicemen were also opened. Even internal mail was censored. If you were writing to your father overseas, you had to make sure you did not mention any of the forbidden topics such as ships or troops. You could be prosecuted for this.

Radio transmission was very closely censored. Microphones in the studios were guarded. Broadcasting of shipping news and weather reports on the radio were banned. This meant that the Air Force would telephone private citizens to ask what the cloud ceiling was in a particular area before sending up its planes. Personal messages and birthday greetings were banned too. Advertisements were rewritten so secret messages could not be hidden in them. Many people listened to Radio Vatican because it gave the names of men who had been taken prisoner of war.

It was not only the soldiers who had to be careful what they said. Everyone in New Zealand was warned that information like shipping or cargo details, location of military camps or aerodromes, weather reports and defence measures might be useful to the enemy.

ssh!

It was thought best that New Zealanders did not hear certain news. An example was when items were going to be in short supply in shops as this could have caused a run of panic buying. Another example was when some of the first furlough (holiday) draft of New Zealand troops from the Middle East refused to return while there were still thousands of fit New Zealand men reserved in industry. This might have caused a loss of morale (cheerfulness) and so the average New Zealander did not hear about it until long after the war had ended.

ssh!

Some events that happened in New Zealand were not published because the enemy would be very pleased to hear them. One example of this were the scraps between American and New Zealand servicemen when the Americans were in New Zealand.

New Zealand was not just worried about its own censorship. The New Zealand Prime Minister sent several cables to the British Government commenting on their looser censorship.

Anything that might upset people was censored. When the police force were unhappy over their rate of pay, this was not only banned from the press but also the Police Journal.

ssh!

Anything to do with shipping had tight security. Wharves were barred to the public. No person was allowed on board a ship without a permit. Customs officers were given more power to search cargoes during war-time. Censorship was applied there too. Books considered to be damaging to New Zealand's war effort were held by the Customs Department.

Don't forget that walls have ears!

Activities

1 You will need a blue pencil or felt pen, scissors, writing paper and a partner to work with.

Write a letter to a friend or relative overseas during the war, mentioning at least five forbidden topics. Swap letters, censor them and return them.

Write a few sentences describing how your letter now looks and how you feel about it.

2 During the war, people argued about censorship. Find out about today's censorship laws in New Zealand. Then talk about these views of censorship –

A *As we see censorship, it is a stupid giant traffic policeman answering 'Yes' to 'Am I my brother's copper?' He guards a one way street and his semaphore has four signs, all marked 'Stop'.* (Adams, 1944)

B *Four hostile newspapers are more to be feared than a thousand bayonets.* (Napoleon, 1804–1852)

C *The hand that rules the press, the radio, the screen and the far-spread magazine, rules the country.* (Justice Brandeis, 1942)

A spy behind every bush

At the beginning of the war, the population of New Zealand was 1,640,000 – 8,000 of these were **aliens** (born in another country). Many were Chinese and Dalmations. There were also some Italians and Germans and New Zealand was at war with Italy and Germany. Suddenly, people began to whisper about spies and sabateurs who might help the enemy by acts such as derailling trains and cutting telephone lines. Such people were called a 'fifth column'.

In New Zealand during the war, aliens were kept under close watch by the authorities such as the police. Special laws were passed about them.

If you were an alien...

...and you were aged 16 years or older, and had ever been a subject of an enemy country, even if you were a naturalised New Zealander, you had to register with the police. You were given a certificate and you had to produce this every time you were stopped.

...and a police officer or a member of the Armed Forces thought that you were not loyal to New Zealand, he could take you into custody. The Attorney General could order you to be interned. (Locked up on Somes Island in Wellington.)

...and you changed your address or name, you had to notify the police.

...you were not allowed to work on a ship or a wharf without a special police permit.

...your mail was closely censored.

...you had to get police permission to leave your home for more than 24 hours.

...you were not to own or control motor vehicles.

...even if you had been naturalised, you were not liable for compulsory military service.

...a New Zealander was not allowed to sell property or lease it for more than three years to you without the written consent of the Minister of Justice.

You had to be given a classification. There were five special classes:

Class A Recommended for immediate internment. Openly supported Nazism or Fascism, likely to communicate with the enemy, likely to side with the enemy if it came to New Zealand, likely to hinder the war effort.

Class B Recommended for internment if invasion threatened. Not quite so open in their enemy support but dangerous and loyalty still in question.

Class C To be restricted to one particular job or home. Not likely to help the enemy but the public is worried about having them free to go anywhere.

Class D Subject to alien laws but not interned or restricted. Either too young, too old or too ill to be dangerous.

Class E Exempt from all alien restrictions. Loyalty is thought to be beyond question.

Posters warning about *loose talk* were put up. Some people complained that others were seeing spies behind every bush.

Children played spy games and wrote coded messages to each other. The simplest one was a code strip done on two pieces of paper –

A	B	C	D	E	F	G	H	I	J	K	L	M	N	O	P	Q	R	S	T	U	V	W	X	Y	Z

A	B	C	D	E	F	G	H	I	J	K	L	M	N	O	P	Q	R	S	T	U	V	W	X	Y	Z	A	B	C	D	E	F	G	H	I	J

so, for example, the word **SPY** becomes **XUD**.

The Japanese Riot

During the war, New Zealand had a prisoner of war camp for Japanese captured during the fighting. To the Japanese, becoming a P.O.W. was a fate worse than death. Some killed themselves because of this loss of face. *Harakiri* was a traditional form of Japanese suicide. When they arrived in New Zealand, they were taken to the camp about a mile north of Featherston in the Wairarapa.

The camp was divided into compounds.

No 1 compound	**No 2 compound**	**No 3 compound**	**Suicide compound**
labour battalion members and camp hospital	men from the Japanese Navy	Japanese Officers	Men who wanted to commit harakiri

Guards – 3 Officers, 104 other ranks, 84 in administration and services.

Date – Feb. 25 1943.

Events – Men from No 1 compound left the camp in a work party. Men from No 2 compound refused to form a working party. The riot started.

Arms – Guards had rifles and bayonets. Japanese had stones and home-made weapons such as hammers, knives, chisels and hammered out nails.

Results – 40 Japanese killed, 82 wounded, 8 more died later. 1 guard killed, 6 wounded. Remaining Japanese were returned to Japan in Jan. 1946.

Japanese P.O.W.s doing paid work, under guard, in a market garden.

Activities

1 Divide your class in half. The first half is the war-time public of New Zealand. The second half are aliens living in New Zealand. Throw a dice to score your classification.

1 = Class A alien
2 = Class B alien
3 = Class C alien
4 = Class D alien
5 = Class E alien
6 = Japanese P.O.W.

The two groups spend some time talking to each other. Then swap round. At the end of the exercise, write a sentence or two about how you felt in both roles.

2 Some people worried that 'disguised' advertisements from German sources could be placed in New Zealand newspapers.

Spy message –

Nazi friends meet Rainbow Park 10 am Saturday

Make up an advertisement for a product with the spy message hidden in it. Then say how easy or hard this was to do and how you expect your *Nazi friends* to be able to recognise and decipher the message.

3 Make up a simple spy code. Swap with a partner and see if you can break each other's code OR share a code and decipher each other's messages.

War-time schools

Because so many students would be in danger in an air raid, it was important for schools to get trenches dug or other shelters organised.

War-time schools were different to today's. Maori students in the country went to schools called **Native Schools**. Most children, European and Maori, got some primary education but only some of them went to secondary schools. To be able to go to secondary school, you had to pass a special examination called **Proficiency**. Even if you had passed, your parents might decide they could not afford to pay for you to go and you would leave school to get a job and earn money to help the family. This meant that the only students in secondary schools were the ones who could afford it and who wanted to go, or whose parents wanted them to go. Many students left school when they were younger than 13 years old.

Cadets were an important part of school life. Boys were taught about weapons, basic military tactics and first aid, compass and map work. They went on marches and had parades. On very hot days, for some boys it was a test to see how long they could stay in line without fainting. Cadets continued on in schools long after the war and most schools disbanded them in the 1960's and 1970's.

Because of war shortages, changes were allowed to school uniforms. Girls could wear socks or bare legs instead of black stockings and boys could wear sandals without socks.

WAR CHANGES

Wider view of world	Free apples to pupils	Milk supplies to schools rationed	Health suffers e.g. malnutrition, skin problems		
Teacher shortages because of war	Free text books for primary schools (1944)	School Library Service began (1942)	Accrediting for U.E. introduced (1944)	School certificate introduced (1944)	
School leaving age raised to 15 (1944)	New core subjects of Maths, Social Studies, English and Science introduced	New subjects like Art, Craft and Music introduced	School Publications Branch set up to produce New Zealand school books (1939)	Regulations for flag saluting on special days and deaths of old boys overseas	Patriotic working bees on buildings and grounds began

Keeping Students Safe

Keeping students as safe as possible was the responsibility of individual schools. There was not one evacuation policy for each school in New Zealand. It was thought, for example, that schools near the coast, in the main centres, or near key targets such as aerodromes and wharves were in the greatest danger. But New Zealand is not a very wide country and so nobody could feel totally safe no matter how far inland they were.

Trenches were dug at schools for pupils to hide in during an air-raid attack. Students would have turns at *hedge-hog duty* which was clearing the trenches before other students got in. Students learned about how effective team work was. In drills, where there was a primary school close to a secondary one, the older students would be put in charge of some younger ones.

Camouflage was sometimes used. In some schools, each student had a sack with a hole for breathing. When the siren sounded for drill, the students filed into the trenches carrying their sacks. Then they put them over their heads and lay down in the trenches, camouflaged. In one school, students hid in an emptied swimming pool over which a huge camouflage net was pulled.

In some areas, mothers sent their children to school with a matchbox containing cotton wool to stuff in their ears and a piece of cork to bite on during an air attack.

In other areas, children were taught to practise screaming as it was thought this would save their hearing being affected by the planes and bombing.

If there was no warning, students were to lie under their desks.

Schools practised *quick home going*. This was to take place if there was enough warning of an attack. Students had to race home as swiftly as they could. Mothers complained that if they could do the trip in five minutes during a drill, why did it take them up to an hour at other times.

Some schools were built on stony or hilly grounds and it was hard to dig trenches. Many students in Wellington and Lower Hutt, for example, were advised to hide in the gullies, parks and scrub on the hills.

Some schools built surface trenches. These were made by putting sandbags in front of banks or walls.

Some students wore identification tags. Various sorts were made.

During the war, some schools lost buildings which were taken over by the Army or Hospital boards.

Activities

1 Write down one occasion you might do the following during the war –

(A) check for hedge-hogs
(B) practise screaming
(C) dive under your desk during a lesson
(D) salute a flag
(E) wear a named disc
(F) sit in a covered swimming pool
(G) stand up for a song
(H) study 4th Form Maths while teacher takes 6th Form Latin
(I) take a match-box to class
(J) practise going home.

2 Design an identification disc that is cheap and easy enough for parents or students to make for themselves.

3 Use a full page to draw the picture of the war-time school.
The boxes marked with a star mean change has taken place in this area during the war. Put a change in.

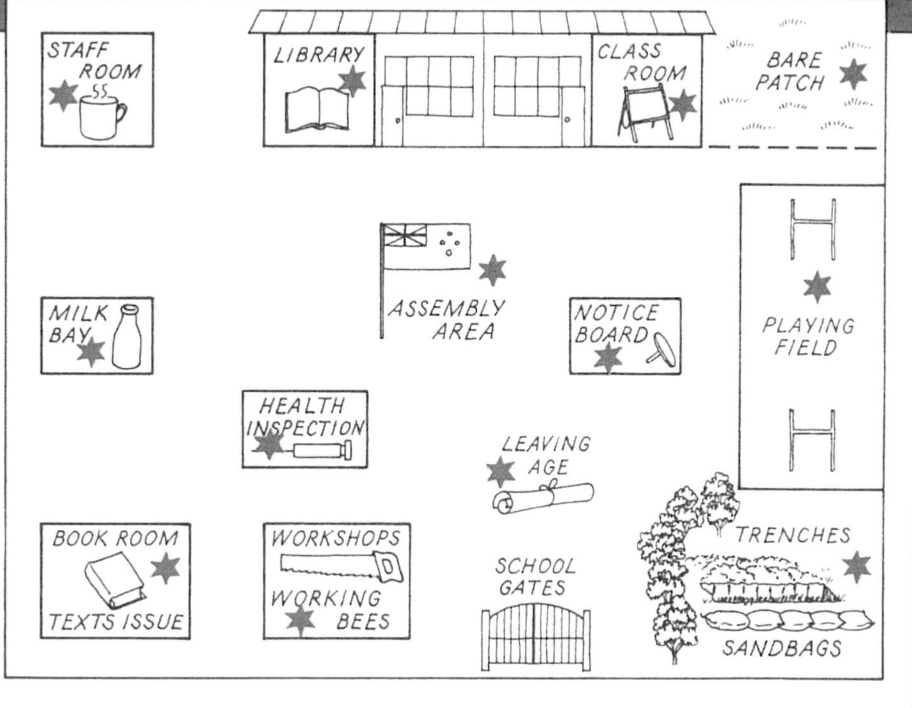

The Maori war effort

In October 1939, it was announced that an infantry battalion of Maori recruits would be formed. Within three weeks, 900 men had enlisted. When the battalion embarked, 32 of its 39 officers were Maori.

Maori were not conscripted like European during World War 2. Conscription for Maori during World War 1 had been very controversial. Many Maori, especially Taranaki and Waikato who had lost a lot of land in the confiscations after the 1860 wars, resented conscription and a group of Waikato had been put in prison for resisting it. So, when the Government decided to bring in conscription in 1940 for New Zealand, Maori leaders pleaded that Maori not be included. Maori girls did not go overseas. Sir Apirana Ngata stopped it.

In 1942 the Maori War Effort Organisation was set up. The country was divided into 21 zones and 315 tribal committees were formed. It was voluntary and did not get any Government money. This was the largest Maori organisation ever set up.

Its main areas were organising –

- recruitment of soldiers
- encouraging food production
- investigating housing conditions
- investigating education, vocational training and land use of Maori
- running 'Basket Socials' which was the auctioning of food kits for patriotic purposes. The Maori Princess, Te Puea, raised nearly £40,000 for the war effort in this way.
- making lists of men and women and recommending war-time jobs for them. They were often called on at short notice to fill labour quotas for certain jobs. In some areas, freezing works and dairy factories could not have operated without their help. On many of the State farms set up to provide vegetables for allied forces in the Pacific, the work was carried out almost entirely by Maori men and women.

All the usual home comforts such as socks, cakes and cigarettes were sent to the men overseas. So were special treats such as barrels of muttonbirds. When the Germans captured some of these, the propaganda minister Lord Haw Haw told the Germans that the New Zealanders were so short of supplies that they had been reduced to eating salted seagulls.

One ancient Maori remedy was very useful during the war. Koromiko, chewed raw, is an excellent cure for diarrhoea and was taken to the Middle East for the New Zealand soldiers.

In 1988, the Army Museum in Waiouru opened a major display on the 28th Maori Battalion. Two special displays shared pride of place. One was the medal group of Te Moana-Nui-A-Kiwa Ngarimu, VC and the other was the canteen truck *Te Rau Aroha*.

Te Rau Aroha means *Offering of Love*. It was the name of the truck which was bought with funds raised by native schools in New Zealand for the Maori battalion overseas. When it arrived overseas, a man called Charlie Bennett was put in charge of it. It was a V8 Ford Truck mobile canteen that served as a meeting centre as well as the place to get everything from toilet articles to hot soup. *Te Rau Aroha* came back with the Maori battalion to New Zealand and toured most of the native schools as a way of saying thank-you.

Activities

1 In 1940, Sir Apirana Ngata defined Maoritanga as "*the inculcation of pride in Maori history and traditions, the retention as far as possible of old time ceremonies and the continuous attempt to interpret the Maori point of view to the pakeha in power.*"

Write out the definition a Maori leader might use today.

2 Find out more about –

- war-time work on the Maori Land Development Scheme
- the Maori Battalion's campaigns
- ti-ti
- Turangawaewae Marae
- Lord Haw Haw
- koromiko (Hebe)

3 Play the Patriotic Game with a friend.

Heads starts. Use the black circle as the place to start spinning a small coin. Take turns.

Keep a note of the squares your coin lands in. Nobody can collect on a square more than once. If you land in such a square, you do not have another turn.

Scoring

inner squares	=	5 points
middle squares	=	10 points
outer squares	=	15 points
coloured squares	=	– 20 points

Total your scores. *The Best Patriot* is the highest scorer.

Use your collected squares to write a few sentences about how you helped the war effort.

Barrels of muttonbirds were sent to Maori troops overseas.

The Patriotic Game

attend the Ngarimu Victoria Cross investiture meeting at Ruatoria to honour 2nd lieutenant Moana-Nui-A-Kiwa Ngarimu 2nd New Zealand Expeditionary Force; killed; V.C. winner	gather koromiko for troops	become a leader of a tribal committee	collect potatoes and pumpkins for Army camps	pack barrels of mutton birds for troops	entertain troops from Army camps each Sunday at Turanga-waewae
	collect pipi for kits	pack parcels for Maori troops	make camouflage nets from green flax	organise a dance for Red Cross funds	
buy a copy of Maori Battalion Marching song and learn it	pack clothes parcels for Britain	weave flax kits	collect mussels for kits	perform haka for official visitors	
decorate flax kits	gather seaweed for kits	organise a Basket Social	fill kits with preserves and salted meats	sell farm produce for war funds	raise funds for Te Rau Aroha
join the 1941 big publicity campaign on radio to get Maori recruits	work in the freezing works		work on a State vegetable farm		mediate (help settle) in an employer-employee dispute at a factory
	join the Armed Forces	work in a dairy factory	farewell reinforce-ments for Maori Battalion	clean up after fund raising on marae	

Those who said 'no'

If you were a pacifist you might be 'sent to Coventry' (people crossing the road to avoid talking to you) or lose your job

Not all New Zealanders believed in the war. Some said all wars were wrong, others that New Zealand should never have got involved in this one, others that it was not right to conscript men for fighting. A general term used for such people was **pacifists**.

Some pacifists tried to get others to listen to their point of view by addressing crowds in the street or a park. People sometimes threw things at them or pushed them over. A band might start playing the national anthem to drown their speeches out. Or people might sing and shout. The Mayor might ask the crowds not to listen to the pacifists. If they wore sandwich boards with slogans against the war on them, someone in the street usually grabbed the boards and ripped them up.

Sometimes people sneaked on to wharves and put yellow stickers on ships and boxes of butter ready to go to England. The stickers had messages like '*Down With Conscription and the Imperialist War*'. Stickers also appeared on lamp-posts. White paint was used for graffiti with messages such as '*No More Troops Overseas*' and '*New Zealand Comes First*'.

When the Government brought in conscription, it was in a difficult position. Some of the people in Government had been against conscription during the first World War. The Prime Minister, Peter Fraser, had spent 12 months in prison on a charge of sedition (making statements against the recruiting of soldiers and compulsory military service).

If a man got 'call-up papers' and did not want to become a soldier, he could go before a group of men called an **Appeals Board**. You could make an appeal on three main grounds – *Public Interest* (you could help the war effort better by staying at your job); *Undue Personal Hardship* (example, helping a widowed, poor mother); *Conscientious Objector* (it is against your conscience to fight). If your appeal was dismissed and you still refused to fight, you would be sent to court as a defaulter. To start with, you would face a £50 fine or three months in prison or both. If you still refused, the Judge would sentence you to a detention camp for however long the war lasted. There were 13 camps with 803 men in them.

Screws are the patrolmen and supervisors.

- no ordinary leave
- no newspapers or radios
- only immediate family allowed to visit
- not allowed to go and work on farms where there is a great labour shortage

- banning your tobacco
- stopping recreation
- banning mail
- bread and water diet
- fines
- a spell in gaol (the boob)
- solitary confinement for 23½ hours per day for periods of up to 3 days (the dummy)

- always served last in a shop
- children bullied at school
- bricks thrown through windows
- neighbours refuse to talk
- wife cannot get a job

Activities

1

I am a conscientious objector

I am a member of the armed forces

Make yourself one of these labels. Choose the one that best represents your view-point.

Walk round the class meeting people with a different label. Exchange points of view.

At the end of the exercise write a few sentences about how understanding of different ideas can be increased.

2 Study the material in and around the 16 boxes on the *Camp Detention Chart.*

Draw up your own 16 boxes to correspond. Make yours 1 cm by 1 cm.

Then put either a red cross or a blue tick in each box to represent these –

Red Cross = areas where you would be subjected to heavy stress

Blue Tick = areas where you would be able to cope.

3 Use *The Camp Detention Chart* to write an account of your time in a camp during the war.

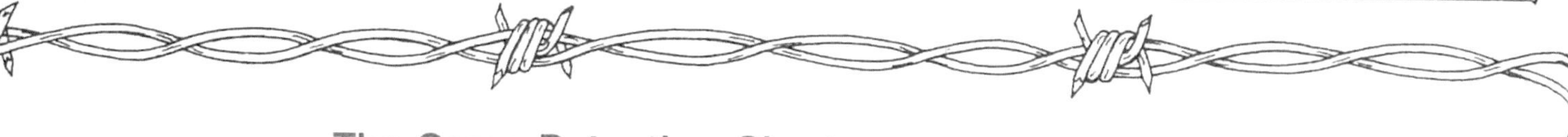

The Camp Detention Chart

- psychologists
- lawyers
- Church Ministers
- farmers
- teachers
- water-siders

Wire happy is when you just sit round all day with your head in your hands because there is no purpose in your life. It could lead to you being transferred to a mental hospital or suicide

- debates
- discussion classes
- drama
- musicals
- card games
- hobby classes
- occasional swim or bush walk

Screws control your life from waking time till lights out at night.	You are mixing with men from all walks of life.	You go through a long period of being *wire happy.*	You have to do something in the evenings to stop boredom.
One of the aims of the camp is to lock you away from the rest of society.	You are allowed two days compassionate leave when your child dies.	Camp food is unexciting but wholesome and adequate.	Your wife gets white feathers in the mail. Your children find them in their school desks.
Discipline is very strict.	The local butcher refuses to supply the camp because of the 'conchies' in it.	You are told even when war ends, you won't be able to vote in elections.	Your problems in the camp range from big to small.
Your wife and children are suffering because of your beliefs.	Routine of 6.30 am rise, cold shower, breakfast, outside work squads set off at 9, finish at 5.	You get paid 13c a day.	You hear how your friends on the outside are accusing you of looking for a *funk-hole.*

White feathers are a symbol of cowardice. The term comes from a white feather on a gamecock's tail being taken as a sign of inferior breeding and therefore having poor fighting spirit

- constant roll checks
- freezing cold winters
- army blankets are thin and holey
- you are not allowed to appeal against your sentence
- you are not allowed to use ablution block after lights out

Work outside the camp –

- grubbing thistle, ragwort, fern
- cutting scrub and manuka
- digging drains
- planting shelter belts
- building roads and railways
- building fences
- weeding and growing flax

Work inside the camp –

- mending clothes and boots
- cutting firewood
- servicing cars, tractors, trucks
- mowing lawns
- growing vegetables
- cooking meals
- working in offices, stores, hospital

A funk-hole is a place you go to escape from something you are frightened of

The same for everybody

SUGAR RATIONED (12 OUNCES PER PERSON A WEEK)

UNPOPULAR WITH HOUSEWIVES BECAUSE OF BIG AMOUNTS OF BOTTLING AND PRESERVING THEY DID

PRODUCTS LIKE CHOCOLATE AND SOFT DRINKS BECOME SCARCE

CAKE SHOPS CLOSE EARLY

GOLDEN SYRUP AND HONEY USED INSTEAD BUT THEY ARE OFTEN IN SHORT SUPPLY

BUTTER RATIONED (8 OUNCES PER PERSON A WEEK)

MARGARINE NOT AVAILABLE BECAUSE AMERICANS USED IT FOR COOKING IN TROPICS

BUTTER SUBSTITUTE = 1 TABLESPOON LEMON JUICE AND A PINCH OF BICARBONATE OF SODA ADDED TO HALF A POUND OF DRIPPING

INSTEAD OF BUTTER ON TOAST USE DRIPPING WITH SALT AND PEPPER

Rationing is a fixed allowance of provisions such as food and clothing per person. Instead of being able to buy as much as you want, you are allowed to buy only a certain amount. This is the same for everybody, regardless of whether they are rich or poor.

New Zealand had rationing during the war. The war interrupted normal shipping and production. Ships coming to New Zealand had first to get past prowling enemy boats. When a ship did get through, and the goods arrived in New Zealand shops, the owners decorated their windows with red, white and blue and hung big posters with slogans such as *Britain Delivers the Goods.* New Zealanders had seen enough of queues during the depression. They had hoped the time for queues was over. But when the goods arrived, queues often formed outside the shops.

Another reason for rationing was the number of men, who used to work at producing goods, now overseas fighting. This reduced production. At the same time, New Zealand was also sending food to people in Britain who were desperate. Later New Zealand also sent food to the American Forces in the Pacific. This meant some foods had to be rationed to make sure there was enough for export.

Sugar, butter, tea and some meats were rationed. Fish, cheese and eggs were in short supply but they were not rationed.

Everybody over 10 years old was given special ration books. They were 13 cms by 11 cms and so were easy to carry. You had to be careful not to lose them because you would not be allowed to buy goods that were rationed without them. Inside were stapled sheets of coupons which the shopkeeper took out.

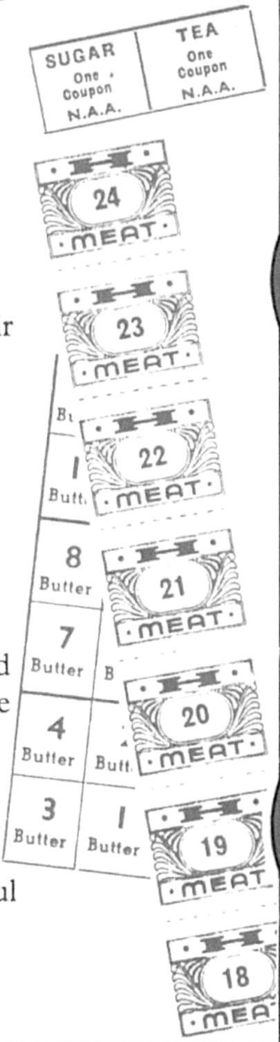

CREAM VERY RESTRICTED

CAN GET CREAM ONLY WITH A SPECIAL PERMIT FROM DOCTOR

ONLY FOR PEOPLE WHO NEED HIGH FAT DIETS e.g. DIABETICS, ELDERLY, T.B. PATIENTS

TEA RATIONED (8 OUNCES PER PERSON A MONTH)

TEA IS THE GREAT NEW ZEALAND DRINK

FEW RESTAURANTS SERVE COFFEE. FEW GROCERS SELL COFFEE BEANS. NO INSTANT COFFEE

PEOPLE WRAP A BIT OF TEA IN PAPER WHEN THEY GO VISITING. CALLED A TWIST OF TEA

OWNERS OF HOTELS, RESTAURANTS, BOARDING HOUSES COMPLAIN ABOUT ALL THE FORMS THEY HAVE TO FILL IN

SOME MEATS RATIONED

NOT RATIONED ARE MEATS LIKE SAUSAGE, MINCE, OXTAIL, LIVER, KIDNEY, TROTTERS, TRIPE, HOCKS, SHINS, RABBIT....

DEMAND FOR MINCE SO GREAT IT GETS RATIONED

COOKS PUT A LOT OF STUFFING IN ROASTS & VEGETABLES IN STEW

PEOPLE GET RID OF PET CATS AND DOGS

FISH IN SHORT SUPPLY

IF YOU WANT TO BAKE A CAKE, YOU HAVE TO PLAN IN ADVANCE AND SAVE THE INGREDIENTS.

NEW COOK BOOKS OF WARTIME RECIPES

SEVERAL BIG TRAWLERS ARE TURNED INTO MINESWEEPERS

HARDER TO FISH e.g. SMALLER BOATS AND BLACK-OUT RULES

LIMITED OIL FUEL

SOME FISHING GROUNDS BARRED TO FISHING BOATS FOR DEFENCE REASONS

EGGS CONTROLLED BY GROCER

FOWL FEED IMPORTED SO IT GETS DEARER AND SCARCER

PEOPLE TOO BUSY TO KEEP HENS

EGGS ARE GOOD TO BARTER WITH. e.g. ONLY A FEW BANANAS COME INTO N.Z. A TOWNIE MIGHT SWAP A FEW BANANAS FOR A BASKET OF EGGS

CHEESE CONTROLLED (2 OUNCES A WEEK)

Strange contraptions began to appear on the backs or running boards of cars. These were to make the petrol go further. There was a gas producer called *Gasogene* which was advertised as the world's best coal gas producer. Sometimes household gas was carried in big bags on the roof. They held about 50 cubic feet of gas but you needed 290 cubic feet to equal 1 gallon of petrol. Other units burned charcoal. None of them gave as much power as petrol. Starting the car could be tricky. Charcoal burners were also very smelly. The driver had to rake out the clinkers (produced from burning of coal) and leave piles of hot ashes on the roadside. This was a fire risk.

Horses made a come-back. Sometimes they were hitched to cars or other unusual looking vehicles made by the owner. Even in hilly Wellington, for example, rubbish collections were made by horse drawn vehicles wherever possible.

Trams and trains were always crowded during the war. Children slept in the luggage racks.

Petrol Rationing

Petrol was the first to be rationed. Cars were hard to get in New Zealand during the war. In 1940, the importing of cars was banned. But by that time, petrol rationing had already started to make a lot of changes to the way people lived.

Afternoon mail deliveries to residential areas ended. Before the war, the postman would deliver mail to the door. Now people put mailboxes at their gate. Householders with no mail boxes had to collect the mail from the post office.

Getting new tyres was very hard. There were a lot of forms to fill out, even for a bike tyre. You had to prove that a bike was the only means of getting to school or to work and you were not cycling for pleasure. Your teacher or employer had to sign a form and a cycle dealer had to inspect the old tyre. Then he had to go to the local rationing authority. If your application was successful, the dealer would be given a tyre to sell to you.

There were a lot of prosecutions for petrol offences such as stealing petrol and forging coupons. The punishments were fines and imprisonment.

If you wanted to use your 2 gallon ration for a Sunday drive, you put 1 gallon into the tank and drove until you ran out. Then you had your picnic. Then you put the other gallon in and drove home.

From time to time, long distance travel was restricted and you had to apply for a permit to go over certain distances, such as 50 miles (80 km).

Activities

1 Make up nine small coupons as shown:

SUGAR	EGGS	MEAT
CHEESE	BUTTER	FISH
PETROL	TYRES	TEA

Decide which article you will collect. Then go round the class and swap. The aim is to collect as many coupons of the same article as possible.

At the end of the exercise, write a sentence about how barter works and how effective at it you were.

2 Become one of the following people and write about how rationing has affected you –

- housewife
- nursery owner
- home bakery owner
- bike owner
- car owner
- waitress
- butcher
- amateur angler
- diabetic

3 Problem Sharing
Write down one problem you might expect to face during war-time rationing. Some examples could be –

- You need a new tyre for your bike but the local rationing authority has turned you down.
- Your grocer tells you he has no eggs but you see him slip some into Mrs A's shopping basket.
- You are expected to have a dinner party to entertain your husband's new boss.
- You need some special ointment from the vet for your cows before milking time but you have used all your petrol ration.

Take your problem to your group and see if you can get it solved.

4 Try making The Victory Roll, a popular war recipe.

The Victory Roll

Mix a pound of flour (either self raising or plain with baking powder) with a quarter pound of suet. Use water to make a stiff dough. Roll out. Chop bacon and parsely, spread over dough. Wrap in greased paper, then cloth, place in pan of boiling water. Simmer for 2–3 hours.

Coping with shortages

During the war many of the things that are freely available today were in very short supply.

War-time Shortages

Timber

Before the war, most timber for furniture had been Japanese oak. Now New Zealanders discovered their own woods such as rimu and tawa. When combs and hair-brushes became scarce, some were made from these woods. The shortage of labour and wood led to furniture controls. The making of items such as plant stands, standard lamps, bookcases and cocktail cabinets was banned. Cabinet-makers had to obey certain rules. They could not make bedroom or dining suites with more than six pieces. Sizes and numbers of tables, tea trolleys, drawers and mirrors were set. There was a great shortage of fruitcases. Apple and pear boxes had to be returned to the growers.

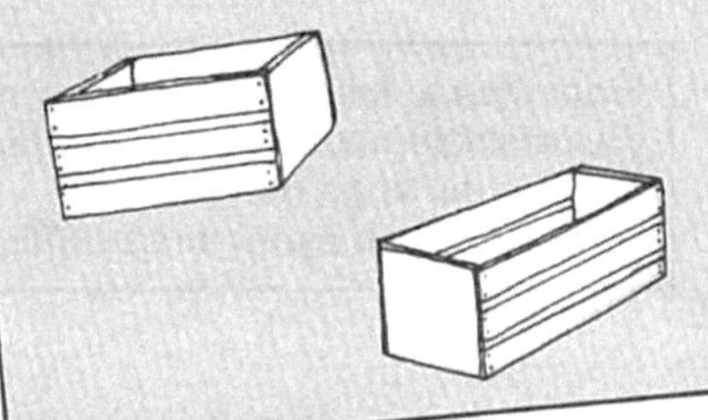

Paper

At this time, most of New Zealand's paper and cardboard came from overseas. This soon became scarce. Butchers and grocers asked women to bring their own paper to wrap their shopping in. Cotton bags or bits of sacking or linen that could be washed easily were used to wrap bread and meat in. The size of newspapers kept getting smaller. A 20 page newspaper might be cut to about 6 pages. Special regulations were passed about paper. You were allowed, for example, to type on both sides of legal documents. The typing was single spaced and the margins smaller. People saved envelopes and readdressed them. People took clean paper to depots for recycling into brown paper. A lot of everyday paper products, such as advertising leaflets, streamers, confetti, table napkins, library book covers, cake frills, hand towels, face tissues, cardboard for packing shirts, were banned.

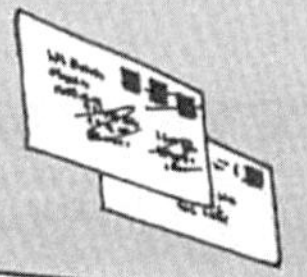

Vegetables

The Government ran a 'Dig For Victory' campaign. People were told to beg, buy or borrow spades and plant vegetable gardens.

Services

Several essential services had shorter hours. Banks, for example, closed early for a while.

Binoculars

On race days, there was always an appeal for binoculars. Patrons were asked to give or lend or sell their race binoculars to the Government for the Armed Forces.

Anything made of rubber

It was very hard, even for farmers, to get a new pair of gumboots during the war. Hot water bottles were kept for sick and injured people. To keep warm, people used to wrap up a brick or stone they had warmed in the oven. Elastic was almost impossible to buy. You had to use buttons and tapes instead.

Hospital equipment

Papier-mache was used to make all sorts of hospital equipment such as slings, trays, splints and basins. It was made from one inch strips of waste paper and covered with waterproof glue. The finished product was so strong it could be used for boiling water. Backing material pulled off rubber retreads before use provided linen for bandages. The material was very stiff so it was smoothed out, torn into standard bandage widths, put into a laundry bag, given a thorough washing and then unravelled. Women took the white covers off their dresses in wardrobes and ripped them up for bandages. Night staff at some hospitals did their rounds with candles and storm lanterns.

Electricity

Labour and material shortages meant delays in hydro electricity projects. At the same time war-time industries were working harder and needing more electricity. This made electricity in short supply at peak load times.
People were asked to switch off lights and radios in empty rooms and cook as much as possible at one time to avoid using ovens too much.
Daylight saving was extended.

Housing and goods

Lack of products meant that houses could not be finished. The frames of many houses were left waiting. There was a shortage of corrugated iron and iron was taken from fences to use on roofs. Wooden spouting and pipes were used. New telephones were banned. Household shortages included cutlery, pencils, clocks, crockery, bottles, needles, watches, razors, shoe polish, golden syrup, kettles, toasters.

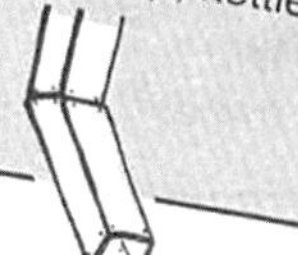

Young people responding to the challenge

Young people helped a lot during the war. They all had members of their family overseas or knew someone who did. They helped collect:

- **old clothes** to send to people in Britain
- **bottles** to pack products in-the usual tins were needed to pack articles for the troops overseas
- **cast iron** products needed for bombs, grenades and other armaments
- **aluminium** for aeroplane building
- **cotton rags** needed for bandages
- **lead** for bullets
- **waste rubber** – needed for a lot of things besides tyres; farmers, for example, needed it for their milking machines and hoses. Anything from rubber gloves, tennis shoes, bathing caps, to bath plugs were all needed. Garages set up huge collection bins. City Councils put special rubber bins on their rubbish trucks.
- **special plants** - Ergot (a sticky fungus on fescue and marram grass that stops bleeding), Agar agar and Caragreen (seaweeds used by industries); Rosehips (used to make vitamin drinks) from Wild Dog Rose.

Industry responding to the challenge

New Zealand industries were able to produce many weapons for the war. Examples:

- hand grenades
- trench mortars
- sten guns
- light armoured cars
- Tiger moths
- Brengun carriers
- anti-tank mines
- jungle knives
- mortar bombs
- grenade mortars
- chemical land mines
- shell fuses

New Zealanders were very good at making products instead of relying on imports that might never arrive. Radio, metal-working and instrument-making industries grew. When a shipment of ball bearings was lost because of enemy action, an appeal for replacements went out all over the country.

Some factories switched goods. A jewellery factory, for example, made air force instruments. A toy factory made ammunition carriers.

New shipyards built –

- steel minesweepers
- powered & wooden barges
- crash launches
- lighters
- tugboats
- ship repairs
- submarine chasers
- refuelling barges
- patrol ships
- flare path dinghies
- steel barges
- wooden wherries
- amphibian trailers
- powered lighters

New war industries were set up, *example* – linen flax to make rope and twine.

Activities

1 Choose one of the people listed below. In your group discuss ways you all could have helped the person to overcome the problems caused by war shortages.

People
- solo parent with no home and three children
- a Hospital Board Chairman
- a builder
- a private Kindergarten owner
- a bored 14 year old

2 A salvage display
Each person is to choose an item to bring for the display from the list of World War 2 *Salvage Items* below.

When the display is completed, write a few sentences about any problems you had and how your display might look different to you than it would have to your 14 year old grandparents during the war.

Salvage items

ointment jar	aluminium saucepan	cast iron wheels	old gumboot
golden syrup tin	a tennis shoe	glass jar	aluminium colander
pair of galoshes	iron saucepan	aluminium baking dish	glass bottle
man's woollen sweater	cast iron scales	a flour bag	kitchen grater
iron kettle	apple box	bathing cap	woman's cardigan
aluminuim salt and pepper service	rubber glove	old library book covers	hot water bottle
old tyre	ointment jar caps	old sheet	used envelopes
pile of old newspapers	aluminium jug or teapot	cast iron saucepan lid	kitchen whisk
pair of binoculars	rubber bath plug	boy's old shirt	aluminium coat-hanger
girl's sweater	a crepe sole	a tobacco tin	some ergot

Special rules for clothes

Before the war, clothes in New Zealand had been very formal. Women wore dresses, for example, not jeans or slacks. They wore gloves to church and social engagements. Girls wore short white ankle socks until they were about 16. Then they got their first pair of fully fashioned stockings. It was as important a day as that when boys got their first pair of long pants. Men and women wore hats. Working men such as butchers or wharfies wore long aprons. The war brought changes to all this.

Activity

1 Design a garment that would have passed the **Austerity Clothing Regulations**.

When clothes rationing started, you got 52 clothing coupons for a year. A new blazer or raincoat, for example, needed 8 coupons.

Clothes had a military look with their plain, tailored lines. Coats were modelled on navy duffle coats and had names like *Jeep Coats* and *Swaggers*. Women were told when victory came, they must have their frocks and blouses V necked. They should embroider special V signs on pockets and so on.

Women, doing what used to be men's work, discovered the convenience of trousers. There was a much increased wearing of slacks by women although even by the end of the war, this was not correct wear in some places.

Brides married in curtain netting, satin lining and parachute silk. Many men and women got married in uniform.

New clothes were made from old ones. Materials were dyed. Home dress making classes became popular. Worn collars were turned on shirts and sheets were turned to the outside. War-time colours were greys, browns and beiges. Women tried to brighten these up by wearing coloured scarves. Headscarves began to replace hats although hats such as pill-boxes and slouch hats were still worn for formal times.

Even material to sew with, had to be bought with coupons. There were some exceptions like baby nappies and some furnishing fabrics. Ticking, a strong cotton material used to cover mattresses, was not rationed and many mothers made pyjamas out of ticking for their children.

A 1465 4th SERIES The Rationing Emergency Regulations 1942

HOUSEHOLD LINEN RATION CARD

These coupons may be used only to purchase blankets, sheets, pillow-cases, towels, tea-towels, face-cloths, quilts, and furnishings.

Name :

Address :

You must present this sheet when making purchases of household linen. Do not present loose coupons, as they are worthless and will not be accepted.

Household ONE COUPON Linen

You must present this sheet when making purchases of clothing and footwear. Do not present loose coupons, as they are worthless and will not be accepted.

Clothing ONE COUPON

In 1942, **Austerity Clothing** started. Austerity means severely simple, not having any luxury or ornaments. Austerity clothing set down special rules for manufacturers to follow to save materials. If they broke these rules, manufacturers could be fined.

Austerity Clothing Regulations

For men and boys

- Shirts must not have double cuffs, pockets, neck reinforcements, laced fronts or more than 5 front buttons.
- Coats must not be double breasted, have belts or half belts, pleats or yokes, unused buttons, more than 4 pockets, flaps or tabs, hems of more than $^1/_2$ inch.
- Sports coats must not have more than 3 pockets, blazers must not have linings or braid, waistcoats must not be double-breasted or have backstraps.
- Trousers must not have cuffs, pleats or extended bands or ankle width more than 20 inches.

For women and girls

- No balloon or leg of mutton sleeves, no capes or hoods or double yokes, except on school tunics.
- For girls over 16 years, hems cannot be more than 2 inches.
- For hip sizes up to 42 inches, skirts must clear the floor by 15 inches, bigger sizes are allowed 5 more inches.
- Slacks cannot have cuffs or pleats or legs wider than 22 inches at hem or hems deeper than $1^1/_2$ inches.
- No bridge coats, wraps or coatees, no suits of more than 2 pieces or with coats more than $10^1/_2$ inches below the waist, dresses not to have matching long coats, boleros or jackets.
- No full length frocks or any beachwear except bathing costumes, shorts, shirts.

The American Marines

AMERICANS LEAVE 1944. DANGER OF JAPANESE INVASION HAS PASSED. CAMPS ARE TAKEN DOWN. BUILDINGS ARE USED ELSEWHERE.

Some social changes brought by the Americans

popcorn	flowers and candy sent to a date	candy scrambles for children
women called ma'am	flowers and candy sent to date's mother	chewing gum
shoe shining	sheaf of roses to say thank you for date	hamburgers
laundry and dry cleaning services	some Sunday openings of sports clubs	Coca cola
book matches	bubble gum	some Sunday movies
	tips for service	

A special 36 page guide book was put out for the Americans in New Zealand. It was called *Meet New Zealand.* One of its articles was a glossary of Kiwi expressions and their meanings.

Glossary of terms

COBBER	SHEILA	JAKE	GRAFT
SKITE	CROOK	NARK	CORKER
DINKUM	A FAIR COW	CHEMIST	UP THE POLE
COCKY	DIG, DIGGER	SQUATTER	WOWSER

Activities

1 Head up a page – **'Glossary'**. Down the left hand side, write the New Zealand expressions from the Glossary supplied and down the right hand side, choose from this list the matching term.

DRUGSTORE	BOAST
BAD	NASTY PERSON
TRUE	A BAD THING
RUINED	HARD WORK
FRIEND	SPOILSPORT
FARMER	GIRL
VERY GOOD	GOOD
NEW ZEALAND SOLDIER	BIG SHEEP FARMER

Then provide a further list of New Zealand slang expressions that Americans meeting New Zealanders today would not be familiar with. Supply interpretations for them.

2 Make your own copy of the **'Some social changes brought by the Americans'**. Colour code it like this –

RED = changes that have lasted
BLUE = changes that have not lasted

Underneath, write a few sentences about how understanding of different cultures may have been increased by the war-time contact.

Grabbed by Manpower

Because the work was so dangerous, there were strict rules about work in munitions factories.

The Government had to organise the work force so that the most important places got enough workers. The way it did this was by a special scheme called **Manpower**.

Certain key industries were called **essential industries**. This meant they were so important it was essential they had enough workers. If you worked in an essential industry, you could not leave or be sacked without the agreement of the District Manpower Officer. If you wanted to leave, you had to give seven days notice.

During the war, a lot of industries were put on the essential list. The first ones on the list were –

- defence construction
- munitions
- coal mining
- hospitals and freezing works
- footwear, woollen, knitting and rubber mills
- timber industry
- railways
- dairy factories
- flax and linen flax mills
- gas and electricity supplies

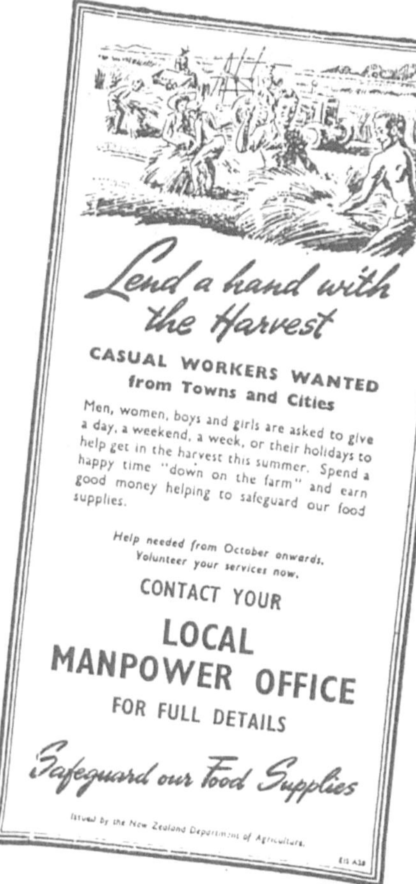

Big demands on New Zealand workers

New Zealand was a Pacific country. It felt it should help fight Japan.

New Zealand's troops in the East needed constant reinforcements.

Britain's need for New Zealand produce was desperate.

American troops in the Pacific needed New Zealand supplies.

November	1941	82,000 in armed forces
February	1942	125,000 in armed forces
September	1942	157,000 in armed forces

New Zealand industries were needed to make munitions and other war materials.

People did not like Manpower. They thought of it as big hands coming out of the blue to grab them. "*Being grabbed by Manpower*" became a common expression.

At any time you could get a letter telling you to go for an interview. Manpower officials tried to match the person with the job but it was not always possible. The result could be that you ended up with a job you really hated. And you might have to travel a long way to get to your manpowered job. Few people had cars, petrol was rationed and public transport was always crowded.

Sometimes, certain ages were called up. An example might be all women aged between 22 to 25 in a certain area being called up to work in a local munitions factory. Generally, women over 40 and most men over 60 escaped the clutches of Manpower. But some industries needed workers so urgently that men from 18 to 65 might have to register at Manpower Offices for them. A lot of young boys and girls worked instead of going to school. They could find themselves working alongside an 80 year old.

Sometimes, it did seem as if Manpower had far-reaching hands. In 1943, for example, beginning in Auckland, all men and women on release from prison, were interviewed by District Manpower officers to give them jobs in essential industries.

If you tried to escape from Manpower, you could end up with a fine of up to £50 or 3 months in prison.

Manpower officers, along with the police, could question people in private homes and in public places like hotels, cinemas or billiard rooms about their jobs and whether they were registered with Manpower. People called these visits by Manpower officers, *raids*. Sometimes, the Manpower officers raided places like tea rooms and golf courses as well.

Activities

1 Study the Santa Claus cartoon.

Rule up a box to show the six Santa figures in the cartoon. Choose one word from the list to describe Santa's feelings. Put them in their correct boxes.

- disbelieving
- disgusted
- calm
- eager
- annoyed
- cheerful
- bored
- furious
- puzzled

2 Draw your own cartoon of someone who has just been *manpowered* into a factory.

3 Nominate one person in your group as the Manpower officer. The rest are possible workers, five of which are needed for a munitions factory. You all have to go before the officer for an interview. He then selects the five.

When you have finished, discuss how the five chosen felt, what excuses were offered and how the officer made his/her decision.

The farming community

War challenges farmers

There is a great shortage of labour.

Import restrictions mean rationing and a shortage of equipment.

If you still had a gun, you could go rabbit, deer and pig shooting to help beat meat rationing.

If machinery breaks down, it is hard or impossible to get replacement parts.

Big vegetable gardens are planted to help beat rationing.

You could run hens. Eggs can be sold, bartered and pickled.

A lot of ordinary jobs like fencing, have to be stopped.

Fertiliser, needed to stop newly broken-in land going back to scrub and bush, is in short supply.

Some dairy farms are near airforce bases. Cows in the shed are frightened by low flying planes.

The war disturbed normal trade. Trade with most of Europe and Asia was severely restricted. Exports to Egypt, the United States and British countries increased. But the Government had been prepared. It had made arrangements that if war did come, New Zealand produce would be bought by the British Government.

To help the farmers' shortage of labour, the Women's War Service Auxiliary organised a special group of women. It came to be called the Women's Land Service and the women who joined it were called **Land Girls**. At one time there were over 2,000 Land Girls.

Their wages varied. Dairy farms paid £1 15s per week plus keep for the first 6 months. After that, wages went up to 22s 6d. On other farms and stations, they got £1 10s per week plus keep for the first 6 months, then £1 15s.

Some farmers' wives who had not had a holiday for years, thought the Land Girls were spoilt because they were supposed to have holidays of not less than 7 days every 12 weeks.

The Land Girls scheme lasted until 1946. At the end of it some women were very pleased to go back to the city. But others had enjoyed it so much, they stayed on the land.

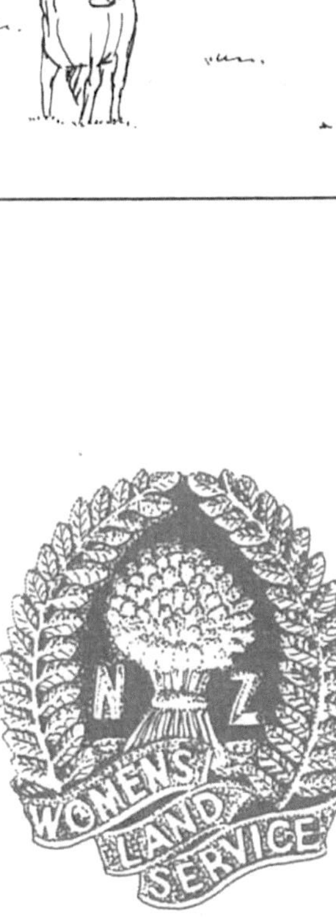

The Land Girls

Some of the jobs land girls had to learn to do –

- fence
- sow crops
- dip sheep
- ride a horse
- harrow paddocks
- clean a cowshed
- shear and crutch sheep
- drive a tractor
- make hay and silage
- milk cows
- run dogs
- grub gorse
- cut scrub
- dock lambs
- garden
- crack a stock whip
- plough
- clear bracken fern
- pull ragwort
- go on lambing beats
- dig ditches
- drain a swamp
- muster
- hand hoe crops
- pluck dead sheep
- get up at 4 am
- help lambing and calving
- mow paddocks

Special State vegetable farms were established to supply the American Forces in the Pacific.

Three special dehydration vegetable factories were built.

Pukekohe	Christchurch	Motueka
dehydrated cabbage and carrots	dehydrated potatoes	dehydrated apples

Dehydration is the removal of water from food without changing its chemical make-up. Just enough water is left to keep the cell structure. When water is added to the vegetables, they swell back to their original size. This is called being **reconstituted**.

Because there is not enough moisture, decay organisms cannot grow and so dehydration also preserves food.

This meant dehydrated food could be taken to the Pacific without spoiling like fresh food would.

Activity

Study the map of the Taranaki area to which you have been sent as a farm worker.

Decide where your farm is and write a few sentences describing its location.

Write out a list of jobs you will probably have to do. Put an asterisk beside the ones you will find most difficult.

Decide how long you will stay (any period from September 1942 to April 1946) and give yourself pay based on the rate for Land Girls.

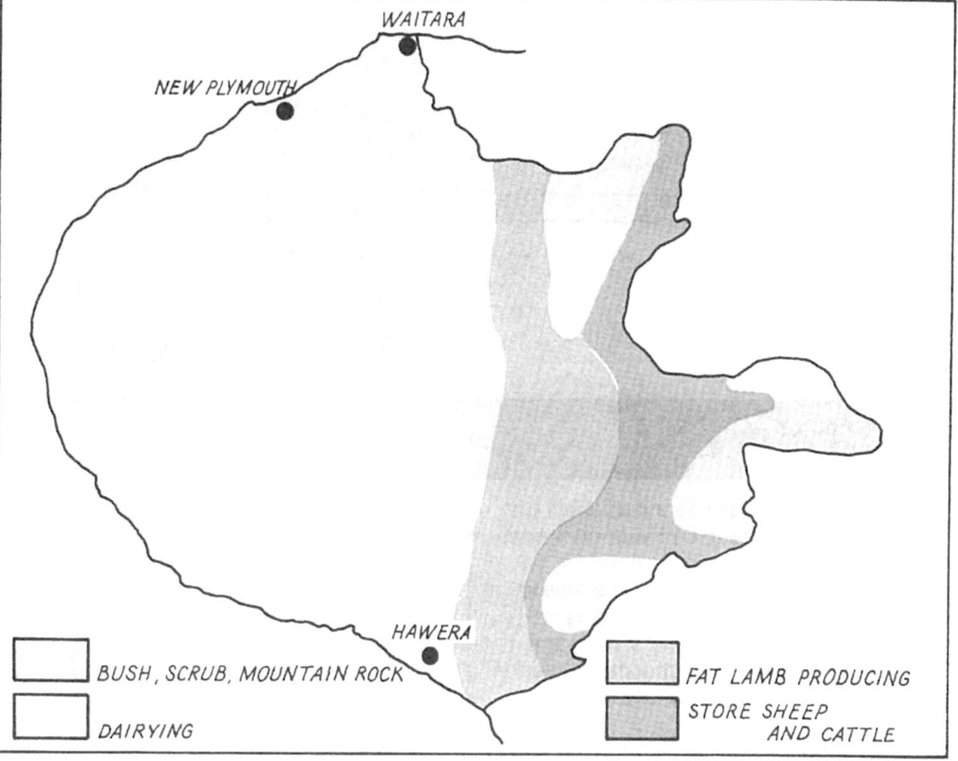

Results of the challenge

New Zealanders' attitudes to the rest of the world changed. Before, there had been a great faith that Britain would be ready to defend New Zealand if invasion threatened. The war shook that belief. Britain was a long way away. New Zealand was a Pacific country. New Zealanders had fought and died in the Pacific as well as Europe. People had still spoken of Britain as being Home before the war. Now New Zealand was Home. This was shown by the popularity of the national hymn, *God of Nations*. It had been around for a long time but copyright had been got for the Centennial Exhibition and it was being used as much as *God Save the King*.

Some New Zealanders had lived through two world wars. They did not want another one. And they had been frightened that Japan had got so close to invading. They became very defence minded and keen for New Zealand to make defence agreements for the Pacific area.

At the end of the war the Prime Minister said that six, long, anxious, worrying, dangerous and tragic years were ended.

On the 8th May Germany surrendered, bringing the war in Europe to an end and on the 15th August Japan surrendere They were called VE and VJ Days.

New Zealanders held VE and VJ Day celebrations. Sirer factory hooters, church bells and car horns sounded continuously. People blew whistles, lit bonfires, dressed up in costumes and danced with strangers in the street. Schools were closed and children wore victory caps and waved vict flags. Victory parades with floats were organised. Shops, streets and cinemas kept their lights blazing. Some shops gave free cakes or cups of tea. There was broken glass fro hotel drinks being taken into the streets and many hotels ignored the licensing laws which said they had to close at 6 o'clock. But it was very hard for women who had lost me during the war to join in such celebrations.

In any classroom, there might have been students at the end of the war with fathers who were –

killed in action	returning unwounded	still listed as missing presumed dead
returning from a P.O.W. camp	returning badly wounded	imprisoned as an alien in New Zealand
imprisoned as a C.O. in New Zealand	had been turned down for military service	going to take up a Rehab. farm
returning unfit for work again	returning to family in a tiny rented flat	studying for a university degree
learning a new trade	going to see their son or daughter for the first time	returning to a wife who wanted a divorce

Winston Churchill said –
"Your country has played a great part. It has never put a foot wrong."

Apart from the Soviet Union, New Zealand had a higher proportion of its people in the armed services than any of the other allies. New Zealand's war expenditure was very high. It was ahead of Australia, Canada and the USA in terms of population ratio. To contribute so much, New Zealanders had been prepared to let their standard of living be reduced.

Casualties

Deaths	11,625
Missing	634
Prisoners	8,086
Wounded	19,345

New Zealand's casualties, in terms of population ratio, were the highest of any allied country except Russia. They received 6,256 honours and decorations including 8 Victoria Crosses.

In 1941 a Rehabilitation Act had been passed to make sure that ex-service-people would receive jobs and housing. No person who had served in the armed services was to suffer any loss of salary or promotion which he or she could normally have expected to get in peace time. Various allowances were made to the ex-serviceman or woman to make it easier for them to cope with fitting back into peace-time.

Activities

1 Make up a questionnaire about the results of war to use in your community.

2 Using the replies to your questionnaire and the text information on changes, prepare either a written or oral assessment about some of the results of war for New Zealanders.

Fashion and peoples' attitudes to it, changed. For women there was a great emphasis on femininity after Austerity Clothing.

Some official war figures

Population of New Zealand in 1939	– 1632,000
Men of military age	– 355,000
Men & women who served overseas	– 135,000
Men & women who joined the forces	– 205,000
Peak number in the Home Guard	– 124,000
Peak number in Emergency Precautions Service	– 150,000

New Zealanders had worked very hard during the war. Girls and boys did shift work in factories. Watersiders worked 84 hour weeks. People worked on Christmas Day. Some industries had a 12 or 14 hour day. It was legal for boys of any age to work on farms. But at the same time, the war helped change working conditions because so many new workers were going into industries. A Holiday Act, for example, was passed in 1944. This said every worker had to have two weeks' holiday a year with pay.

New Zealand forces won a lot of friends during the war. If you travel to places like Greece and Crete today and say you are a Kiwi, there will always be someone in the villages who remembers the New Zealand soldiers and will make you specially welcome.

The war affected unemployment

Year	**Jobless** (thousands)
1938	34
1939	19
1942	2
1945	1

Children were pleased they could have marmite on their sandwiches again but although rationing began to wind down, it did not end immediately. And world economies had been damaged so much during the war, that for many years afterwards, there were still shortages of some goods.

The war caused great people movements. New Zealand men and women went overseas. Wives sometimes shifted to be closer to their husbands in military camps. Workers moved into industries. A lot of Maori left their rural maraes to work in towns and cities.

The war changed some beliefs about male and female relationships. Women had got used to their war-time jobs. When the men returned, a lot of women lost those jobs and while some of them were pleased to return home, others stayed in the work-force in different jobs. The traditional male jobs such as heavy engineering were soon taken over again by men. Women did not stay in those war-time jobs. But nor did they go back to being servants. War meant the end of domestic service. Girls who used to become servants had had the opportunity of doing much more interesting work. What had changed was society's attitudes to women working. The idea of equal pay for women had also won a lot of support.

Women had gained more self-confidence and independence during the war years. Before the war, the wife might have been happy to let her husband make all the decisions but when he came home from overseas, he often found a person who insisted on sharing decisions. The war had changed him too. He might have been physically or mentally damaged. Relationships were often strained. Many men who used to go hunting with their mates before the war came home and never touched a rifle again. Sometimes they might not even be able to bear the smell of fireworks.

It was often hard for the children as well. Some had lived with relatives while their father was overseas and mother doing war work. Others were suddenly confronted with fathers whom they had never seen before.

A Jerry Christmas and a Jappy New Year

START Your father celebrates Father's Day by deciding to enlist. 1

People rush to the shops in panic to buy basic food stuffs such as sugar. 2

Your mother gets you to bury the silver tea service in the garden in case of an invasion. 3

You and a friend are caught trying to make a jam tin bomb. Punishment is no supper for a week. 4

Your best friend's father is missing, presumed dead, overseas. 5

A pacifist in the park is pelted with food scraps and knocked off his soap box. 6

You help pack an emergency ration box for your family. It is too heavy to carry. 7

Your cousin is invalided home in a hospital ship. H[e] has had a leg amputated.

You join an Emergency Precautionary Services exercise as a runner. 26

25

Your young brother and sister get free apples at school. 24

Your little brother falls into a slit trench and breaks his arm. 23

Your school is having a lot more phys ed lessons than it used to. 22

You take eggs to the grocer and earn enough to buy the family groceries. 21

You get news tha[t] your uncle is a P.O.W. in Crete. 2[0]

You help build a mail box to collect mail and milk from your front gate. 27

You try bubble gum for the first time. 28

Your neighbour's husband is a C.O. Someone sets fire to her garden shed. 29

The local Home Guard have got proper uniforms at last. Your uncle skites about his boots. 30

31

You help pack a special parcel for your father in the Middle East. 32

There are rumours of a Japanese submarine prowling your coastline. 33

Your 16 year old brother is workin[g] alongside an 80 year old in his timber job. 3[4]

52

You see your first gas mask and hope you never have to wear one. 51

You help your mother make blackouts out of old rugs and blankets. 50

Darwin has been bombed again. There are rumours of the Yellow Peril landing. 49

An Italian from your area has been interned on Somes Island. You think he is a spy. 48

Your cousin's plane is shot down in the Pacific by the Japanese. 47

You remove a str[ip] of corrugated iron to repair a leak in the house roof. 4[6]

You go to a public demonstration on how to deal with an incendiary bomb. 53

The cast iron collectors call. You give a kettle and a fire grate. 54

A new exam called School Certificate is introduced to schools. 55

56

You make a special Christmas card for your father and sign it Jerry Christmas and a Jappy New year. 57

An old boy of the school has been killed. A special service is held for him. You all salute the flag. 58

Your sister is manpowered into a munitions factory. 59

At last a letter from your father. It has been mutilated by the Censor. 6[0]

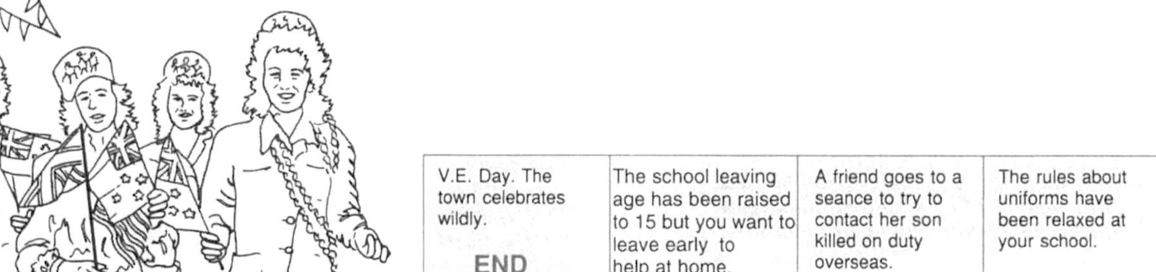

V.E. Day. The town celebrates wildly. **END** 76

The school leaving age has been raised to 15 but you want to leave early to help at home. 75

A friend goes to a seance to try to contact her son killed on duty overseas. 74

The rules about uniforms have been relaxed at your school. 73

You swap some vegetables for some honey. 7[2]

A Jerry Christmas and a Jappy New Year

Rules

- Play with a friend.
- Spin a coin for moves.
  Heads = 2 squares
  Tails = 3 squares
- Make a note of all your landing places.
- Even numbers are worth 5, uneven are worth 10.
- There is a bonus of 20 for finishing first.
- Circled numbers are lucky. Collect an extra 10 for each.
- Walled squares are unlucky. Miss 2 turns.
- When you have finished, use your total and squares to write a few sentences about some of the things that happened to you.

You are given the job of clearing hedgehogs from the trenches before drill. 9

Your school rugby teams are all coached by women teachers. 10

Great excitement because your family is getting a new radio with a magic eye. 11

Your elder sister breaks her engagement to her fiance overseas and marries another man. 12

You spend your holidays working on your uncle's farm. (13)

The army won't take your brother because he has a heart murmur. He gets sent white feathers. 14

You practise evacuation. You are in charge of three children from the primary school. 19

You enjoy the special art and music lessons your class is now having. 18

God of Nations is used as New Zealand's national anthem. 17

The country is in mourning for Savage who has died. The new P.M. is Fraser. 16

You get caught spying on the Home Guard training with their wooden rifles. 15

You have not heard from your Polish and Canadian penfriends since the war began. 35

You win a kit filled with smoked mussels from the fund raising at the marae. (36)

At last you get a new tyre for your bike. It saves you an hour getting to and from school. (37)

Your grandmother shares her cream ration with you. 38

You put a new handle on the spade so that you can dig a family vegetable garden. 39

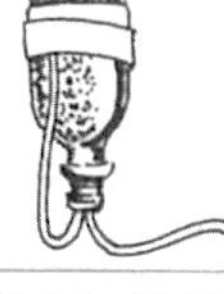

40

45

A friend was involved in a bar scuffle between American marines and some Maoris. 44

Your local hospital appeals for blood donors. Your aunt and mother go. 43

A cousin is sent to Canada under the Empire Training Scheme. 42

You use the last of your precious film on a photo of your father who is home on furlough. 41

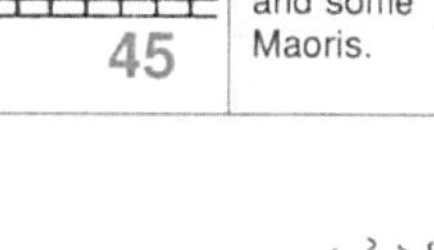

Your local garage owner has been sent to prison for petrol fraud. 61

The family is down to its last hot water bottle. You have to heat bricks in the oven instead. 62

Your mother is unhappy because she has just used the last of her elastic supply. 63

You realise that you have forgotten what a real cake tastes like. 64

You get blisters from cutting the lawn with a scythe. The hand mower is unable to be mended. 65

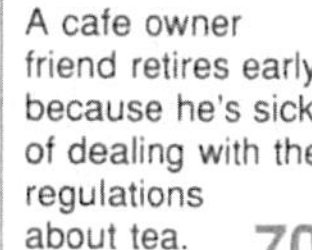

66

71

A cafe owner friend retires early because he's sick of dealing with the regulations about tea. 70

Your aunt dies of T.B. Your cousin is in another special T.B. ward in hospital. 69

Your 83 year old granny is learning to spin because she can't buy knitting wool. 68

The young ones are allowed to sit up to listen to a Winston Churchill speech. 67

A New Zealand response to challenge

The war was one of the greatest challenges that New Zealanders have had to face.

New Zealand was influenced in its response by its attitude to Britain.

There were precautions to ensure the safety of New Zealanders, *examples* – censorship, black-outs.

Organisations were set up to work for the comfort of the forces overseas, *examples* – The Patriotic Fund.

There were measures to help Britain survive the war, *examples* – food and clothing parcels.

Organisations were set up to work for the safety of New Zealanders, *examples* – E.P.S., W.W.S.A., H.G.

People remember the war years as a time when different sections of society, working for victory, all had a common aim. There was a lot of sharing and helping. The idea was that they were all in the same boat and the best way they could help the fighting forces was to get on with the job with as little grumbling as possible.

New Zealanders made sacrifices to help the war effort. A very large number made the greatest of all by giving their lives.

There were measures to back up the fighting forces, *example* – Manpower in industry.

Different beliefs had different reactions to the war effort, *example* – conscientious objectors.

The war changed some traditional beliefs, *example* – working women.

The war helped change the way New Zealand saw itself, *example* – its dependence on Britain.